Gloria —

A Student's Memoir of Intended Paths

PRISCILLA JACOBSON

WESTBOW·
PRESS
A DIVISION OF THOMAS NELSON
& ZONDERVAN

WestBow Press books may be ordered through booksellers or by contacting:

WestBow Press
A Division of Thomas Nelson & Zondervan
1663 Liberty Drive
Bloomington, IN 47403
www.westbowpress.com
1 (866) 928-1240

ISBN: 978-1-4908-4954-6 (sc)
ISBN: 978-1-4908-5380-2 (hc)
ISBN: 978-1-4908-4955-3 (e)

Library of Congress Control Number: 2014915429

Printed in the United States of America.

WestBow Press rev. date: 09/23/2014

MUCH LIKE JOURNALISTS THERE ARE many people, behind the scenes, who deserve credit in encouraging the publication of this book. First, I want to include special thanks to Melinda (Mindy) Kunkel who confirmed, "Gloria has left you with everything you need. Read the e-mails – you have the story.

I am very grateful to Dustin Geralds, of Westbow Press, who believed in my memoir, during a telephone conversation, before putting the words on paper. Dustin emphasized, "You are indebted to this professor, and to readers who need to know how important it is to have someone believe in you. We wouldn't be having this conversation if it weren't for Mrs. Noble."

Jackie McAvoy, who God has used in missionary works, around the world, and today I am privileged to sit with Mrs. McAvoy in weekly bible studies. Jackie has kept me in her prayers and envisions,

"I see you someday talking…yes talking to young people – to students about this wonderful professor."

Thanks to Mimi Landaverde who reminds me of a shower of God's blessings, often overlooked, in the most unexpected places.

Mimi once said, "This book...I believe...will be a blessing to at least one other person."

Most of all, an extended thank you goes to Kathy Duvall who understands the value of both professors and their students. Dr. Duvall states, "I'm glad you had the opportunity to get to know Mrs. Noble. This is your story – you own this experience. Press on!" Dr. Duvall, you are an encouragement to me more than you know.

In Memory Of Gloria Noble

CONTENTS

PREFACE

THIS IS A MEMOIR OF how one professor, and her student, made a unique connection in each other's lives. I intended to write an interview style book about Mrs. Noble. Unfortunately, she passed before I had that opportunity. No comments from desired additional interviews – only the sound of her voice in one treasured interview, a copy of Mrs. Noble's autobiographical sketch, and two years communicating making that prayer-filled connection of encouragement and...hope.

My hope is, professors and students, who someday will be too young to remember Gloria Noble, will feel as if they know her through this memoir. Keeping her memory alive as the chapters unfold through one student's unique story hopefully will persuade professors to value their students and students to appreciate their professors.

Professors and students may enjoy a rewarding experience, learning from one another. Maybe this story will remind students of one of their professors whom they haven't thought about in years. Professors may wonder, "Is there a student out there whom I have made a lasting impression?" The answer is yes! Probably more than you'll ever know.

The Christian audience will be inspired by insights revealed through this story about unforeseen ways that God puts the right people in the right place at the right time. I'm certain there will be readers who will read my story and reflect upon their personal experiences. Others who have disregarded experiences as mere coincidences may rethink: "Is there any such thing as a coincidence or…maybe it could be an opportunity to make a difference or perhaps a testimony? It is vital to seize the moment allowing God to use us to be an influence toward one another.

It can be an enriching experience staying connected to those we care about who are battling a terminal illness. Relating to this, there may have been times you felt that you haven't offered enough. Missed opportunities? Something you wished you'd said or done? Never, look back without giving God the opportunity to remind you what you have given – probably more than you'll ever know… least on this side of eternity.

Yes, there is grief that comes with losing someone special, but there is so much more to be gained by the friendship that is shared.

If you've ever shared a friendship, that others are unaware, it can be disheartening when some discourage the significance God has placed on your experience. I'm confident this memoir will glorify God. This memoir is intended to encourage readers abroad to conquer fears, pursue potential, and appreciate who God puts on your path. I wholeheartedly believe Gloria would be pleased with it. It is in her memory.

One thing no one can take away – your memories...your experience. There are two things I hope to accomplish, a professor to be remembered, and a book to make a difference.

Gloria Noble encouraged me to pursue my dream in writing. She cared for her students and had a remarkable gift for teaching. Mrs. Noble gave me confidence and courage in public speaking.

I overcame a fear of delivering a speech because rest assured – she'd be sitting in the back above the audience listening. Gloria Noble – an aspired reporter/journalist took a detour on the path to teaching. I remember her describing it as a road less traveled by. Mrs. Noble has achieved a greater purpose. She led a life of significance in teaching. Her Opus will live on through her students she has greatly inspired.

Now that Gloria again takes a road less traveled by – it's the most important road. I believe the Lord will bless her and will reward her greatly.

I'm thankful to have been blessed by getting to know Gloria Noble. She was more than a professor – but a mentor and friend. I will greatly miss her and will never forget her. I know Gloria is loved by many people.

I didn't know she passed until two weeks after her funeral when her daughter e-mailed me with the news. I went to the cemetery to pay respects explaining to the lady in the office, at Golden Hills Memorial, I was her former student. She showed me where Gloria Noble is laid to rest – In the Garden of Prayer. I briefly shared my story with her of how she had been such an encouragement to me. She commented: "I love hearing stories like this. I can tell she has had a mighty profound impact on your life."

Now I'll share my experience with you about a speech, a symposium, and…a serendipitous path. Oh, and this is a story to impact, inspire, and leave a lasting impression of good influence in reading about *Gloria*– a student's memoir of Intended Paths.

CHAPTER ONE

It All Began In a Speech Class

I T ALL BEGAN IN A speech class and worth the two years I waited to learn under Mrs. Noble's instruction. She was *the* professor I could truly talk to, giving me the confidence I needed at the time – just to get through delivering a speech. Some professors use other methods by demanding that students get in there and learn by doing.

However, Mrs. Noble's method was flexible and she adjusted to the student's needs. Mrs. Noble was the speech lifeguard who provided me the life-line I'd need to communicate effectively by reassuring: "You'll be fine." She had that special touch providing the extra edge maximizing the speaker's confidence. Mrs. Noble interacted one-on-one, and she cared for her students.

She was warm and friendly, people-oriented, and connected well on a personable level. Somehow, Mrs. Noble sensed what it took to pull out the best in her students. I know she certainly pulled out the best in me.

Speech is one class that is highly critical to get the right professor for the student. Especially, if the student is shy, timid, or self- conscious of any kind of speech impediment however mild it may be. Reflecting back, I'm grateful I pursued what I feared most – public speaking.

Mrs. Noble sent an e-mail two weeks before class began.

> Hello all.
>
> Welcome to speech class for the fall. Please print the attached document and bring it to class with you on the first day. If you have any questions please let me know. Enjoy what's left of your summer!
>
> Mrs. Noble

I replied to her message requesting an outline and the due-date for the first speech.

Mrs. Noble, kindly responded: "I have attached the first assignment. Promise me you won't panic."

It was vital to keep the pace with Mrs. Noble. I couldn't afford to fall behind, so I made certain I stayed ahead of her assignments. I was not a natural in public speaking. The sooner I had my speech written – the more I had time to practice.

I sensed something important about this professor. Maybe it was her high-professional profile, or her optimistic drive. It could have been her credibility introducing herself on the first day of class.

"Allow me to introduce myself and share with you a little bit about my background. I'm Mrs. Noble. Welcome to speech class this semester.

I'm assistant professor of speech communication, instructional technology coordinator, and I was awarded Speakman Excellence in Teaching in 2004."

More important, I realized her sensitivity from her e-mail assuring me not to panic. Her optimism, personable character, and connecting one-on-one was more valuable to me than her credibility. Later, I would discover her award-winning credibility as a journalism professor.

The first assignment began with a brief introductory speech mentioning a few favorite things and something personally descriptive reflecting our personality. Truth is… *I was in sheer panic*!

I'm grateful she provided me an opportunity to get an early start in preparing for the first speech. It took a lot of brainstorming, and with high speech anxiety, I couldn't have put this together on short notice.

First impressions are not always accurate. She seemed to be a privatized individual very focused, typing vigorously on the computer [far right of stage.]

Studying Mrs. Noble carefully I thought: "It looks like she may be difficult to please." Mrs. Noble had a serious, very directive, expression. A profile of someone who knew where she was going in life…and her students better know where their directions are leading them. Mrs. Noble didn't appear to be the type to play around. I had already dropped speech class twice. This was my third try…and now accepting the fact this *is* a talking class – better start talking now.

I introduced myself to Julie who sat behind me and over to my left. "Hi, I'm Priscilla…and your name?"

This mature woman professionally dressed well groomed with long black hair, slightly curled at the ends smiled: "I'm Julie. Have I seen you somewhere before?"

I briefly replied: "I don't recall so." Julie added: "I think I've seen you around on campus."

Trying to keep the conversation a float, I mentioned: "Boy! My palms sure are getting sweaty." Julie laughed: "Do your palms sweat like that in all your classes?" Nervously tapping my pen, against the table, between my fingers replied: "No…just in this class. Sweaty palms reserved for this class only." Julie and I were the only two students in the classroom – we arrived early.

I glanced at Mrs. Noble, and noticed she did not look up to acknowledge our presence. Guess I was hoping Mrs. Noble would ease the tension by participating in our conversation. However, she immediately warmed up, at the end of class, introducing myself to her.

"Hi, I'm Priscilla. You sent me an outline for the introductory speech so I could get started." She glanced up and smiled: "Oh yes…I remember who you are now.

We'll be starting the speeches next week [whispered] don't tell anyone I want it to be a surprise."

Mrs. Noble was attentive to non-verbal body languages – often revealing a student's apprehension. Mrs. Noble, standing in center-aisle, stepping down the staircase [paused momentarily], glancing back as she motioned for the students to come down and occupy the first three rows. Mrs. Noble: "I can tell by the resentful expressions on your faces you're reluctant to occupy the front seats. I can always tell my most apprehensive students by where they choose their seats."

Flanagan 156 was an auditorium-size classroom. Long slightly curved tables filled both sides of the room separated by the staircase in the center-aisle. The first row of seats, from the podium at center stage, was just below eye level. Each row was about two steps above the row in front setting a stadium view looking up overhead at the empty seats above the audience. Behind the podium displayed a huge screen showing our power point presentations.

The students gradually began filling the first three rows. Mrs. Noble emphasized: "Most people fear public speaking more than – death." However, she wasn't about death. Mrs. Noble was optimistically a challenge-seeker and full of life that showed in her confident upright posture and lit-up expression in her eye contact.

Next to the wide double-doors entering the classroom was a sign posted with an arrow pointing down toward the wastebasket: "Negative Comments Go Here."

I don't recall her commenting negatively about anyone. As the semester progressed, Mrs. Noble and I developed a close relationship that I'll always look back and treasure.

Mrs. Noble stressed: "Three…is the magic number." It is vital to mention the three most significant things, in a speech, the audience will remember. The bible could not be mentioned, because it wouldn't be considered a credible source to people in the audience who may be Non-Christians.

Mrs. Noble taught to consider the audience's diversified views when giving a speech. Later, she confided: "I was trying to provide a protective environment."

This was a high performance high anxiety entry-level class. The speaker can control the speech, but cannot always control the audience's response. A negative response from the audience may hinder a timid speaker and shatter confidence from speaking before an audience again. Pre-approval was required before the speech was presented – no surprises.

I asked, "Is it all right if I mention my favorite Christian author, Max Lucado?"

Mrs. Noble kindly nodded; therefore, allowing me to nudge the door open inviting God into this. The fact she acknowledged God by honoring my request convinced me there was something good about this professor.

I believe my opening line in the introductory speech hit off a connection between us. *"Success isn't achieving your goal, but rather pursuing your potential."* We were both pursuing our potential. Mrs. Noble was returning to graduate school pursuing her doctorate, and I was returning to college after fifteen years. We both held professional occupations and also non-traditional students

One of the visuals I brought to the introductory speech was *The Bell Tower* year book from 1995 when I graduated from the LPN program at Ridge Ford University in Arkansas. I had no clue about her background. I didn't realize until after I finished her speech class and noticed [in *The Bell Tower* yearbook] a photograph of Gloria Noble appearing on channel **5** news when she was a journalism professor.

It was probably a good thing I was unaware of her background. I was apprehensive enough in public speaking. Not knowing just who it was I was presenting my speeches to, I interacted with Mrs. Noble on a common level. She could detect where I needed to smooth out rough edges, in delivering a speech, and would work with me from there.

She mentioned prior to this introductory speech, "Don't look frightened at your audience or they'll look frightened right back at you. You'll have your audience worried for you." I didn't have a frightened look, but my audience was worried for me.

Julie was giving me a worried "C'mon you can do it!" expression. My main dilemma was lengthy pauses in trying to cover up stammering in repetitive syllables. I struggled with this speech impediment all my life and only had a small circle of friends who would speak for me.

The only problem was this protective environment hindered the exposure and confidence in public speaking. Sometimes it would get frustrating when a person would ask me a question and someone would answer it for me. This is why speech was the most dreaded class I signed up for. Now it was my turn – for my voice to be heard.

Five minutes I would speak and the audience would listen. I wasn't use to people taking the time to listen. In the silence-filled auditorium, thoughts quickly flashed through my mind: "I don't belong up here *please God get me through this*!"

Suddenly… in a moment's crescendo, confidence spurred, I cut loose when I came to the part flawlessly spoken, "A song that would describe me is Reba McEntire's hit song *Is There Life Out There*?"

I suddenly glanced up at Mrs. Noble. She kicked back in her chair, clasped her hands together, and grinning ear to ear.

I'll never forget her expression more award-winning than a standing ovation – a snapshot frozen only in memory. Gloria Noble believed in my potential – and me. After all, there I was performing in front of someone who could have been destined to be a reporter/ journalist.

CHAPTER TWO

A Speech Worth Giving

I F I CAN SAY ONE thing to influence and persuade one person in the audience – *that's* a speech worth giving. Again, topics had to be preapproved. Mrs. Noble expected her students to pick five possible topics. We were to brainstorm the topic selections – no list to choose from. She would pick among the five each student proposed. I e-mailed her to request a pre-approval. For this persuasive speech, I had my heart set on one topic – Ronald Reagan.

Mrs. Noble,

"I have a very heavy work schedule the week before the next speech. I only have the next two days to work on it. I really have my heart set on one and would like your feedback. I'm requesting to do one on the three attributes that made Ronald Reagan a Great President. Visionary, Character, and Teachable mentioning great achievements under each attribute.

The persuasive nature would be to mention the importance of voting for the person rather than the party. Please let me know what you think."

Priscilla, – "I would like for you to simplify your approach this time and focus on ONE clear persuasive idea with main points that clearly support that idea. For example:

Persuade us Ronald Reagan was a visionary (main points would prove this to us) [Note; some in your audience are too young to remember him.]

Persuade us Ronald Reagan was a man of character (main points would be exampled that proved this to us.)

Persuade us to analyze each issue, candidate etc…on its own merits rather than voting my party.

Does this make sense to you? Let me know what you think."

Mrs. Noble

P.J. "I think I can do that."

G.N. "Great just let me know which one you decide on."

P.J. "I'll probably go with character."

G.N. "Yay!"

Character is a subtle way of inviting God into a speech. She obviously liked the idea of choosing character. Mrs. Noble and I were close to the same age. Both of us experienced *The Reagan Revolution*.

"Many of the students are too young to remember him" gave me the opportunity to speak first-hand representing the generation of that era.

Mrs. Noble gave me confidence and courage in public speaking. I didn't want to mess up this speech. The message was too important. I would be quoting from Ronald Reagan the Great Communicator.

She stressed three simple techniques, breathe – project – inflect. Never once did she mention she had noticed where my words faltered; although, I'm certain she did pick up on these flaws. Her method would soon pay off building my confidence – as a public speaker. I'm convinced most of this is in how the professor perceives the student. Because Mrs. Noble believed in me she was able to pull out the best in my weakest area and surface that hidden potential.

She taught that speech was like driving a car. Does one think when they drive? No need to think about what you're going to say because you already *know* what you're going to say. Just think three things breathe – project – inflect.

With only two weeks to practice on this speech titled: *Reagan a Man Who Valued America*. Arguing with her: "I'm a writer – not a speaker."

"I'm a thinker – not a talker." Mrs. Noble persistently assured, "Hang in there! You'll do fine."

Practicing and trusting her speaking techniques made the difference, making notes where to breathe after certain phrases and… projecting as if talking to someone in the back of the room. Inflection improved performance, setting the pitch, and helped with getting away from a monotone effect. The speech writing process also helped build confidence.

The speech outline was complete within two days and approved. Unfortunately, Mrs. Noble had to take leave for a few days due to a family emergency. She made it to class on Monday the 18th but uncertain if she'd be in class on Wednesday to hear this presentation. Would this mean failing the class? Her substitute had commented, in her absence, "This speech isn't going to fly."

He expected an argument comparing President Reagan with another President. Overpowered by intimidation and feelings this professor did not acknowledge a student's opinion when he asked: "Are you trying to tell me Reagan was the *only* President who could end the Cold War!? No other President could do this? I can tell you right now what Mrs. Noble is going to say."

He didn't know she had already approved and confirmed: "Looks good!" Mrs. Noble wasn't informed of the conflict, but assured her I was very uncomfortable doing this speech in her absence.

Looking back, I'm sure he was a good professor – he just didn't know the circumstances. If only he knew my struggle in speech class, maybe we would have had a more positive perspective of one another. A year later, I interviewed Mrs. Noble only to discover he was the professor who persistently urged Mrs. Noble to teach at the University.

Mrs. Noble replied: "I totally understand. I will do my best to be there Wednesday. Right now, it's unpredictable day to day."

It's also unpredictable how the audience may react to politically persuasive presentations. This was a speech I almost didn't give! However, I built the courage into giving it a try, in her possible absence. Why? A speaker becomes indebted to the audience. The students had commented on the audience analysis questionnaire pertaining to how well they knew Ronald Reagan, and if they would like to see a future president with his values. This speech was no longer for a grade. It was a matter of principle – if *one* person, in the *audience*, is *influenced…that's* a speech worth giving.

Julie was one student I got to know from the first day in class. About a week before my presentation, she gave me a 3x5 index card with a message I continue to read before making a presentation.

"Priscilla, God gave me this verse. It always helps me to remember this before a speech. 'Don't be afraid of a soul. I'll be right there looking after you.'" (Jer 1:8. NIV). God puts the right people in the right place, at the right time.

I was extremely nervous wondering if Mrs. Noble would be there. I glanced in the windows through the double-doors. Students occupying seats, from the previous class, conversing with one another, checking evaluation sheets, and…Mrs. Noble – nowhere in sight. I sat back down at one of the study tables outside the classroom reviewing my speaker's notes and…a quick prayer. Glancing up, just in time, to see Mrs. Noble suddenly show up from around the corner where the vending machines were located. She saw me at the study table… yes in sheer panic.

Her eyes optimistically lit up her expression with her gestured smile. Without a word exchanged, she must've been thinking: "This is going to be a dynamic speech!"…as she was walking briskly past the study area, she confidently swung open the door entering the classroom. All I could do is look up… relieved. "*There is a God.*"

Soon as the students were leaving the previous class, I hurried into the auditorium. Striding up the steps up to about the sixth row, where she sat over the audience, and handed her a copy of my outline requesting to be first to present. Doing my presentation first, there was no time to get nervous, or compare my speech to other presentations. Afterwards, it was relaxing to enjoy listening to everyone else's speech.

Mrs. Noble instructed me to go down to the computer and load my power point. It was still a bit early, and students were gradually making their way into the classroom taking their seats. Ronald Reagan appeared up on the big screen.

I looked down through the class window above the computer screen to see the opening slide visible on the huge screen behind. A student blurted: "Yeah right – he was only an actor." I dared not look up, but looked long and hard at President Reagan to get a good lasting mental image of him.

We used a clicker to advance our power point slides. Instructed not to look back at the screen but maintain eye-contact with the audience. Glaring down onto the computer screen when Mrs. Noble approached in front of me, she leaned over the computer affirming: "Look to the person in the back of the audience…and don't forget to breathe. You're going to do fine."

I stepped up to the podium, on the other side of the stage, the power point in full view, embracing a deep breath of history as it rolled into the present moment. Mrs. Noble motioned for the camera man to cue when he was ready as she returned up to her seat.

A quick glance at the card Julie gave me and laid it down on top of the podium, the cameraman's finger points with the quick shout "GO!" Looking up [not into the lens] but to Mrs. Noble, because rest assured she was sitting in the back above the audience listening.

*To read a copy of the speech see appendix A.

"Look to the person in the back of the audience." The person in the back of the audience was no other than…Gloria Noble. She attentively listened to this speech, taking notes on her laptop and looking up, with the same sincere expression of seriousness as I had getting the message to the audience.

Mrs. Noble was impressed with this speech. She knew when spoken words faltered – writing flourished. However, this time the delivery of the speech flourished – the performance flew! Thanks to Mrs. Noble and her gift for teaching – not a word faltered!

Mrs. Noble's comments: "Outstanding opening impact! You really got our attention and made us want to listen to you." One of Mrs. Noble's talent for teaching, she made her message clear – I was worth listening to.

She was someone who intently listened. This in turn gave me the confidence in public speaking. She reinstated: "Wonderful introduction! Your creativity is marvelous and you gave us good reason to listen to you."

Mrs. Noble added: "Outstanding thesis statement! Very clear, precise, and effective. It is easy to know your position exactly." The thesis statement: Ronald Reagan's character of integrity, duty, and hope set the stage for America's future.

Likewise, Mrs. Noble's character of integrity, duty, and hope also set the stage encouraging me to pursue the utmost potential. Little did I realize at the time I presented this speech it would lead into further research to be presented in the symposium a year and a half later.

Again, she emphasized: "Terrific preview! We know exactly where you want to take us. Keep it up!" I had no idea that I would keep it up and hang in there as this project progressed.

Little did I realize, during my introductory speech, holding up the Bell Tower yearbook, I would be presenting a Reagan speech in front of the Bell Tower. I had no idea, at the beginning of the semester I would even be presenting a speech about President Reagan.

I submitted this speech to the college magazine and was invited to present it at the Bell Tower precisely one year to date from the symposium on April 13th, 2011. I had no idea this was the ground breaking work of research, not yet conducted, or that I'd be presenting Ronald Reagan and Mikhail Gorbachev in the Undergraduate Research Symposium April 13th, 2012.

I kept Mrs. Noble posted:

Dear Mrs. Noble,

You may want to tell your students that giving speeches can be addictive. It felt great! We had a small audience, but I noticed this guy, around our age, walking along the sidewalk behind the audience. I'm sure he could hear me from the distance through the loud speakers. I used him as my focal point, as he stood there attentively listening, while I was quoting the part on Reagan's Brandenburg Gate speech.

I was hoping you could've been there, but I'm sure you're busy wrapping up the semester. I just wanted to let you know your teaching methods last beyond the classroom!

Mrs. Noble replied:

"Oh Priscilla sounds great! I had to run my husband to the doctor for a cut but he is okay! Sorry I missed it!"

I wondered about this fellow, passing by apart from the audience, who suddenly took notice. I maintained direct eye-contact, as if he were the person of importance projecting this message to. Could it be possible he may have been a veteran? I carefully studied his attentiveness.

Could this speech have reflected memories…good memories of hope – of freedom? May be it took him by surprise possibly thinking: "Today…almost thirty years later…Reagan's speeches could still be heard at a university in front of the Bell Tower." I'll never know who this fellow was. Sometimes you never know the importance of who you may be influencing.

It is absolutely fascinating giving a speech sharing historical events from an era I lived in. Witnessing televised events, as the end of the Cold War unfolded, captures the memorable enthusiasm bringing life and meaning to the message. Mrs. Noble emphasized: "It's important to get your message to the audience."

Most students were too young to remember Ronald Reagan, making the message more vital to reach the audience. Ronald Reagan's legacy was something they really needed to know.

The audience was impressed with the presentation – both in speech class and again at the Bell Tower. One student, in speech class, commented he liked the part about how President Reagan's persistence to do the right thing had a positive outcome. He added: "What I'll remember most about this speech is the next day ten-thousand German students sung *"The Star Spangled Banner"* in perfect English" (*An American Life* pp. 383). I firmly believe for outcomes to have a positive and lasting effect it takes someone uniquely special to believe in you.

Thanks to Mrs. Noble –she was the one person who made it possible for me to present this speech. She not only believed in the speech…she believed in me. After all, she believed I was worth listening to.

Gloria Noble was more than a professor – I'll always think highly of Mrs. Noble, she genuinely cared. We had a unique connectable way of communicating. She possessed expertise credibility – likewise she was worth listening to. Furthermore, I looked up to Gloria Noble as my mentor… just as she believed in me – I believed in her.

CHAPTER THREE

A Credible Connection

MRS. NOBLE WAS THE ONE professor I ultimately challenged. She was also the one professor I most admired. However, a deep concern lingered, from her comment at the beginning of the semester, pertaining to the bible and its credibility. Of course, she was referring to students who may be Non-Christians. Keeping curiosities to myself, rather than bluntly inquiring about her views, a better idea was to write a thought-provoking persuasive paper.

Toward the end of the semester, she asked the students to write a conflict-resolution paper. This was the perfect opportunity to express beliefs. When Mrs. Noble commented: "Yes, I was trying to provide a protective environment." She didn't reveal this until shortly after I interviewed her a year later. Meanwhile, I somehow sensed she was a believer in God.

Her character and compassionate personality silently yet profoundly glorified God. Unfortunately, professors are in a conflicting position when it comes to expressing their beliefs. In some situations, their profession hinders them from openly confessing God to their students. Mrs. Noble didn't hinder me from opening the door, inviting God into my speeches in a subtle way.

Mrs. Noble was having a difficult semester with family emergencies. Sometimes a student could rub her the wrong way due to the stress she was encountering. I certainly didn't want to be one to give the wrong impression. Therefore, it seemed awkward to explain to her I believed God put her on my path for a reason. Not only did she give me confidence in public speaking, but she confirmed I had a natural gift for writing.

She had been such an encouragement to me, and I wanted to return the favor through words of encouragement. I understood she had to cancel classes at times, but she always made it to the speech presentations. So, I seized the moment hoping to influence, inspire, and give her the encouragement she needed through this conflict-resolution paper.

Conflict Resolution

The step to conflict resolution that's the most difficult for me is setting criteria in determining the best solution. The reason why is because not every ones' criteria is the same.

I believe people determine their criteria by life experiences, values, and convictions. Not everything is always in black and white, and on the other hand – some things are. Is it better, to make a rational decision…or a right decision? I believe in other persons' freedom to voice their views, and I may not have respect for the view itself, but will have respect for the person.

Two examples I would like to include are what I call Fallacy of Fairness. "If I do for one, I'll have to do for everyone." I believe true fairness is mercy granted in unique circumstances.

The other example is judging people's circumstances and set backs against equal criteria. Who are we to judge that which may be of no freewill compared to that which is of freewill? In other words, life can throw unexpected detours and shouldn't be judged solely from a logical cause and effect criteria.

Personally, I hold strong to virtue ethics. Virtue ethics may not always have a rational-type of criteria, often meets with adversity, and seldom attracts popularity. Often people throw away what they believe for sake of convenience or fear of conflict. The stronger one stands for what is right (even against opposition) will often later discover their convictions paid off. Standing for what you believe may have a high price at first, and even seem hopeless, but the rewards are looking back without regret, and having faith for the future… ***there is one.***

I believe the best way to approach differences is to "agree to disagree". That way both individual's views may be expressed and both persons can leave the conversation still holding on to his/her view. Listening to diversified views, may shed some light on the way we see things and clarify possible misconceptions.

A final thought… against what criteria do we set our decisions? Whose criteria is it? Where does criteria originate? I believe it's vital to have sound and reliable standards, but does the credibility really **have** to be proven?

The ultimate challenge was trying to prove my point in the bible's credibility. In other words, does God really **have** to be proven?

Those who are Christians – God would certainly be the most credible source. Since Mrs. Noble didn't reveal her personal beliefs or convictions, I persuaded from a double meaning perspective. For example, faith for the future…**there is one**, may refer to this life, or as I implied, eternal life. We can't help unexpected detours. I knew Mrs. Noble couldn't help the difficult time she was having during the semester. I hoped she would realize her students understood she couldn't always be there for everyone all the time.

The last week of class, she gathered our papers, and silently proof-read each student's paper during class. Julie, Brianna, and I were discussing how much fun we had in her class. Mrs. Noble turning the previous page face- down, and began reading my paper, then…

she looked up at me with the most bewildered thought-provoking expression I had ever seen!

It was as though we were connecting through communication without being directly outspoken. Her questioning eye contact vividly revealed this. In other words, mysteriously as if there was a spiritual connection between us. Unable to break eye contact, from her suddenly stunned look, left me wondering, what could she possibly be thinking?

I wouldn't know until a year later, when she gave me a paper she wrote a year and a half before mine – we were experiencing a cross-road connection. Mrs. Noble and I encountered each other's paths, at a moment in time, fulfilling God's purpose in both our lives.

My paper was intended to encourage her during her family's current crisis. However, it would hopefully later prepare her for her own crisis on the road ahead.

God indeed put Gloria Noble on my path with a confirmation I was intended to be a writer. At the same time, I believe God put me on Gloria Noble's path with a confirmation to encourage her as she would all too soon encounter an unexpected detour.

God intervenes in unexpected detours. He sends the roadmap revealing His plan for our lives. I'm certain Gloria was a God-send. The semester came to a close. During finals week, I e-mailed Mrs. Noble.

Mrs. Noble,

"I realize you're busy during finals week grading papers. However, I want your honest opinion. I'm at a crossroads in making a very important decision in changing my major to writing. Do you think I have the potential to become a writer?"

Her reply precise and direct in making her point,

"Yes I do. Go for it!"

Did Mrs. Noble notice the creative-writing style in the conflict-resolution paper? Could that have been the paper that set off her response for me to *"Go for it!?"* I wondered if she understood what I was really saying in the paper.

I couldn't get over her deep thought provoking expression, with questioning eye-contact. Of course, I didn't understand this connection until later. Our writing comparison intertwined clarifying its' meaning regarding our paths. Mrs. Noble could compare my paper to hers, I didn't know this at the time; however – she knew.

Although, at the time, she may not have known the road ahead, she could see how our writing correlated.

On the last day of class, I wrote a letter to her explaining my paper, so there wouldn't be any misunderstanding.

Mrs. Noble,

I want you to know, I appreciate you. Professors need to hear more often what it means to have someone like you to believe in their students. The persuasive speech was a speech I almost didn't give.

I had to talk myself into presenting it in your possible absence. If there's something you believe in strongly enough, you become indebted to your audience. If I can say one thing that can impact one person in the audience…that makes it a speech worth giving.

Mrs. Noble, when you showed up, I thought to myself - ***"There is a God!"*** That brings me to explain the conflict resolution paper.

It's written to give the reader (whatever their circumstances) a message of hope and encouragement. It's designed to give an overall view of what's really important. For example, just because something isn't proven…doesn't mean it isn't true.

You mentioned things have been difficult for you this fall. My intent was maybe there would be a line or two that would be of some hope and encouragement for you. Thank you for encouraging me to hang in there – you do the same…and God willing things will get better.

Sincerely;

Priscilla

I became indebted to Gloria Noble since she made such a profound impact – a difference in my life. She was the one person, in the audience, my convictions were driven to persuade.

I don't recall her openly talking about God; although, later I would discover she too was a Christian.

I cannot overemphasize speech was the most dreaded class I signed up for, yet turned out to be the most enjoyable…and the most memorable. I returned to college pursuing a business degree and Mrs. Noble inspired my potential, which in turn, my path shifted to writing. If I didn't pursue this opportunity – I may look back with regrets not knowing the potential that could have been. It took faith in God and faith in Gloria Noble's confirmation.

My path shifted, creating a turning point, setting out to new adventures. Christmas break was a rough time to change majors – most classes full, and a lot of professors were difficult to reach. Kyle Faulkner, the head of the English/Communication department, was in his office days before Christmas on December 21st.

He has an extremely outgoing personality, big smile and a very positive nature. If you're having a bad day – hang around him…thirty seconds, and his positive aura will contagiously magnetically attract. He is a lot like Mrs. Noble – a go-getter. I didn't have an appointment, yet he took the time to tediously complete the task of completing the paperwork needed to change majors. Unfortunately, most classes were full.

We were searching for an open class, any class…interrupted by a phone call, while he was talking, I held up a finger to draw his attention, and quietly whispered as he nodded to my gesture: "I'll be right back." Before he was interrupted by the phone call, struggling to find an open class, he suggested I major in organizational leadership which would only require thirty more credit hours to complete and added: "Least you'll have a degree." I shook my head thinking no I'm not going to sell myself short – no deal.

I responded, "No, I really want to get a writing degree." My thoughts reflecting to a scripture in the bible,

"A city on a hill cannot be hidden. Neither do people light a lamp and put it under a bowl." (Matt. 5:14-15 NIV).

Saved by a phone call interruption, I rushed out to get the speech papers from Mrs. Noble's class there on the seat of my car.

"Here are some writing samples I have from Gloria Noble's class." Shuffling through several papers, glancing over main points – his focus attentively drew attention to the one about Reagan. He responded: "This is good stuff. This is some really good stuff! And you did this in Gloria Noble's class?" Responding: "Yeah…and got an A." He put the papers down and looking up: "If you got an A in Mrs. Noble's class – I don't question anything you do."

"Well let's see, here's a textual research methods class open – oh… it requires a prerequisite in editing, and you haven't had editing. I'll tell you what…I'm going to go ahead sign an over-ride, and put you in research class."

I mentioned, "But I don't have the prerequisite. I don't want to get in over my head, and I want to make an A." He assured: "Don't worry, you will – you're ready, you're definitely ready, trust me." I asked: "But don't I need to get the professor's permission?" He responded: "No, no…*I* – just gave you that permission, you're signed up for the class."

This is the first time ever I had been signed up for a class by consent prior to having a required prerequisite… and an upper-level class.

I e-mailed Mrs. Noble eager to share the good news.

"Yesterday I changed my major to Rhetoric/Writing. I spoke with the head of the English/Communications department and he seems to like my writing. I'm really excited about this! He put me in Textual Research Methods (per consent.) I will truly appreciate if you put in a good word for me. I've done everything I can to talk myself out of this.

I question it, and don't know where this will lead. I have a passion for writing and…I believe it's time. I honestly and whole-heartedly believe I made the right decision. I've waited two years to be in your class and it was well worth the wait.

I believe God puts the right people in the right place at the right time. If this is what He [God] wants me to do, it'd be a waste and wrong not to pursue it. Thank you so much for your encouragement and…yeah, I'm going to go for it! I'm really going to miss your class and hopefully I'll get good professors."

Mrs. Noble replied: "Thanks so much. You will do great I'm sure of it!"

CHAPTER FOUR

Research Begins

The Two Must Work Together

I N THE SPRING OF 2011, I began textual research methods. We primarily learned to think organically. In other words, expanding on a previously written paper and going deeper into the research. The Reagan speech was perfect! It gave me the opportunity to research the Cold War. I narrowed it down to the Reagan/Gorbachev years in ending the Cold War.

I learned to create a file, and type a summary [annotating] what I read. Citing each source, was the saving grace in later knowing where the sources came from in preparing for a long research paper. There were two basic kinds of sources – secondary [other people's research] and primary [first- hand information.] Starting with secondary information is valuable in finding out what other researchers are saying.

However, I wasn't impressed with the analysis the researchers were concluding about Ronald Reagan.

First, it was too analytical and missing the point of who Reagan was, what he believed in, and what he desired to accomplish. I saw the movie *The Reagan's* numerous times which gave me a great idea for the Reagan speech. *The Reagan's* revealed Ronald Reagan's personable character. The analysts were studying causes and effects in historic events rather than studying the people.

It was also important to use a variety of sources. For example, in addition to the data-base – books were also a good source. I purchased several books written by authors who knew Reagan and Gorbachev. Although their opinions varied, authors who lived during this era and knew these two leaders would be closer to getting to a primary source.

Kathy Duvall, my research professor, curiously made the comment, "I want to know your research method."

I was puzzled by her statement: "How do I explain this…method?" I wasn't thinking of a method – I was having fun. In response, "I… well…play it by ear." Dr. Duvall boldly questioned, "You don't mean to tell me you wait for that serendipitous moment!?" I replied to the truth, "Yep."

After her comment, serendipity took the lead. Through my research, it was one serendipitous moment after another.

My method? – Serendipity.

Dr. Duvall, shaking her head in amazement at all the archived information, "Priscilla, I've never seen anyone research like you." Dr. Duvall advised I needed a sponsor who specialized in political science. I explained to her this research began as a speech in Gloria Noble's class. She agreed I speak first with Mrs. Noble then locate a sponsor.

I made an appointment with Mrs. Noble, and we briefly discussed the project. She readily stated,

"I would sponsor you, but I don't have a category. However, I'll be willing to work with you on the presentation, and…you presenting, [glanced over her glasses, with a confident tone], I'm not worried about it."

Did she mean "I'm not worried about it" referring to how much I had progressed in her class…or, that she knew I wasn't a perfect speaker, and it didn't matter to her? Either way she meant – it really didn't matter. I knew she had confidence in me and I took this as a compliment.

I was registered for fall classes including a political science class. Mrs. Noble suggested I speak with Dr. Yarborough about sponsoring me. Mrs. Noble sent me an e-mail: "Tell him I will co-sponsor."

I made an appointment to see Dr. Yarborough. He was impressed about the Cold War topic. He stated,

"I've never seen a project like this presented in the symposium! This is very unique – something that has an ongoing research potential."

We both agreed the Cold War contained useful research to include politics, history, science, military, foreign policy, and presidents. He implied I studied enough about Reagan and the answer would be found in Gorbachev. I begged to differ; although, I knew it would be important to study both men equally. I knew little about Gorbachev. A lot of Americans wondered about the intentions of this Soviet leader. I remember seeing Gorbachev televised, giving speeches in Russian and interpreted in English. Back then, some people wondered, would he be the one to start a nuclear war? I further researched with the positive notion…any friend of Reagan is a friend of mine.

Dr. Yarbrough and I discussed the thesis statement. Character and values…he questioned, "Character and values does what?" with a smirked grin. Was he taking me seriously?

Intimidated by his reaction, I answered: "Makes great things happen?" He stated: "No, it has to be something simple. Don't worry we don't have to decide on a thesis today." However, I was determined to stick with character and values.

Dr. Yarborough, highly intelligent, yet very analytical, was using what he called an XY theory. This was making things more difficult than it had to be. Why not keep the presentation simple? Finally, after much thought, why couldn't I have told him character and values ended the Cold War?

I felt that he was trying to lock me into an XY theory to disprove my thesis. Later, I would discover he took my research more seriously than I initially gave him credit. The greatest accomplishment that day, he agreed for Mrs. Noble to come aboard as co-sponsor.

Mrs. Noble and I were the two who worked together, closely collaborating, through this entire project. Gloria Noble, an aspired reporter/journalist, possessed a multi-talented gift.

Reporters and journalists must be able to communicate on several levels. They speak to people of all ages, all education levels, and people from all walks of life. Mrs. Noble communicated from both a sophisticated and a common level. She was very clear and directive, encouraging, flexible and…fun.

Mrs. Noble kept the project exciting by encouraging me to have fun with it. She had a natural gift for teaching. Mrs. Noble wasn't distant – she got involved taking a keen interest in this project. Her optimism sparked my enthusiasm. This in turn gave me the drive and persistence to hang in there. We were a team, and I had the desire to please her as I progressed with this project.

It all went back to Gloria believing in me and confirming,

"You'll do great I'm sure of it!"

I wasn't about to let her down.

It was a tedious summer collecting annotations from a variety of sources, and spending countless hours going to the campus library daily researching the archives. However, I hoped to locate a primary source for an interview. Dr. Faulkner and I met, in the parking lot, on the way to campus.

K.F. "Hi Priscilla! How are you're classes going?"

P.J. "Oh, I pulled out of summer classes to focus solely on this research I'm doing for the Symposium. It's about the end of the Cold War – the Reagan/Gorbachev years. I'd really like to find a primary source to interview."

K.F. "Hey – I'll give you a wild and crazy idea – how 'bout interviewing Gorbachev!"

I jokingly accused him of being sarcastically funny,

"Yeah right."

K.F. "No, no I'm serious. When politicians retire they're searching for opportunities to speak on college campuses and meet with the students."

I did accomplish getting a reply from Mike Duggan [chief archivist] from the Reagan Foundation. Mr. Duggan offered to help me find a primary source to interview. I went to the provost with my idea. They couldn't figure out what I was doing – giving me a stunned expression – that I'd be inquiring about getting a primary source to come to campus. Guess it's not every day a student marches into the provost with an optimistic adventure like this. The people from the provost were very polite, but just didn't know who to direct me to... this was taking me around in circles to the next person and back to the previous one I spoke to.

Again, it was important not to get discouraged. I couldn't lose valuable time needed to move on with the research project. It was a useful strategy working simultaneously on two main themes. One theme was the Berlin Wall, and the other Star Wars.

I knew Reagan's mission, over the years, was to somehow...*"Tear down that wall."* I was partial to the Berlin Wall theme knowing it was Reagan's passion. However, it was difficult to get Reagan and Gorbachev to interact on the Berlin Wall topic.

The only way to accomplish this was to do flash-backs and flash-forwards of meetings between Reagan and Gorbachev. My introduction focused on the night the Berlin Wall was built...in six hours! (dir. Halmburger).

Mrs. Noble replied, "Hello Priscilla,

I'm sending this back to you with some comments. Let me know if the comment bubbles don't show up. In general, you have some great research in here, but I don't want it to sound like a history lesson, SO,

I would suggest you take this content and place it in the form of an informative (or persuasive- depending on what you actually wish to accomplish with this) speech outline. That will force you to remember your audience, AND limit your content to the relative materials only. Then we can go bad and place it in the form of a narrative if you like and I can help with the audience member's perspective. Make sense?"

I thought so highly of Mrs. Noble and appreciated the time she was taking to help me with this – I didn't waste time arguing. I let her do the directing and…I'd just go for it.

I told her, "Sounds great. I can do that."

Next, I edited the narrative and shaped it more into a speech. I sent her another draft.

Mrs. Noble,

"This is a more edited one in a speech outline format. You're right, it does make a difference. The narrative feels like reading out of a book. Let me know what you think, and any suggestions on polishing it up more."

Just short of five hours, Mrs. Noble responded quicker than the Berlin Wall was built! "Hi, I've read this – I need to see you in my office. When are you on campus?"

I quickly made an appointment with Mrs. Noble the next morning at 8 a.m. Frantically worried thinking: "Is she going to get on to me? God *is* in this.

The outline contained Reagan's and Gorbachev's one on one meeting where Reagan used an analogy, "I'd like to fix my son a gourmet dinner, have him sit down and enjoy the meal...then ask if he believed there was a cook." (Reykjavik File pp. 9). I also added: "Both these men acknowledged they were not alone." In other words, implying God was moving through them.

I had no idea how she would react, and having peer review phobia, walking into her office sheepishly grinning, "Heeeyy." Mrs. Noble repeating the greeting: "Heeeyy. C'mon over here and sit down. I want to go over a few things with you.

First, we need to work on some clarity." Sitting on the other side of her desk, Mrs. Noble invited,

"Pull your chair over here and sit beside me, so we can look at this draft together."

Pointing to the top of the outline Mrs. Noble commented,

"You said Ronald Reagan challenged the fall of the Berlin Wall. Let's change this to Ronald Reagan challenged the existence of the Berlin Wall."

Explaining to her, "That's actually what I meant."

She replied, "I think what's happening here is, you can do too much research and get a brain overload."

I inquired, "I don't understand why this is so difficult. It was so easy to put the Reagan speech together in your class. Now, I'm being taught to research, and pick my thesis from my research instead of forming the thesis first like you taught."

Mrs. Noble suggested, "You need to take what they tell you with a grain of salt, and do what works best for you. I like to pick the thesis first, and research behind the thesis statement. Sometimes, you may have to change your thesis but not necessarily."

I also added, "Another problem is I quote a lot because I have plagiarism phobia. I know I need to learn how to paraphrase more."

Mrs. Noble confessed, "I have the same problem with plagiarism phobia. I like to quote a lot too. My professor is always getting on to me 'Gloria, you quote too much.'" I glanced back and forth at the Reagan speech outline and the Berlin Wall outline laying side-by-side on her desk. Mrs. Noble broke the momentary silence, "You look like you want to say something."

I responded, "I'm just thinking…do you think I ought to expand on the Reagan speech?"

Mrs. Noble answered, "That's totally up to you…but [pointing at the Berlin Wall theme]…I think you really want to go with this one."

I picked up my papers, determined to give this another try, closing the conversation as I started to leave her office, Mrs. Noble grinned, "Priscilla…I know how you think." One thing Mrs. Noble made vividly clear…she didn't edit, not one thing pertaining to God.

I was still uncertain about what Mrs. Noble believed. However, I made certain she understood what I was trying to do.

Mrs. Noble,

"I'm really stuck on getting the clarity, but I can see where you're coming from. What I'm trying to do is, take something big and bring it to this level. For example, there's a symposium about Reagan at Regent's University with a panel of speakers. I don't fit into their caliber or credibility, but I want to be able to do more than just what the symposium requires. I didn't slide by in your class and made an A. The only way I know to write it with clarity is…Who was Ronald Reagan…really?

What was this guy all about? He didn't fit the political profile. He wasn't analytical, but what did he stand for?

I've been hesitant to ask because I don't know if they'll let me use Reagan's beliefs about God and providence. I think that's where my clarity is diminished in my rough draft. I know there will be people who will agree and disagree, but that's all right. I'm not trying to push what I believe, nor what I think the audience ought to believe…it's what Reagan believed.

Mrs. Noble… you've really encouraged me in both public speaking and writing. I really appreciate the time you're taking to help me with this project. Let me know what you think."

Mrs. Noble encouragingly responded, "Priscilla – ultimately, it is your project and I want you to be happy with it, so pick your directive and…Just Go Girl!"

"Just Go Girl" – an expression rarely heard from a professor. Gloria Noble wasn't just any professor, she was supportive – sticking by me, inviting the challenge, and loyal in seeing it through. I sensed she was having fun with this, and…adversity only sparked her determination.

Determined to get this message clearly to the audience, I read the presentation to my daughter, and much to my surprise, I had to share this story with Mrs. Noble.

Mrs. Noble,

"Rough drafts can be humorous. I tested this on my 24 year old daughter. She really didn't get it. She said, "I didn't know Ronald Reagan could cook. His son would probably say, "Dad…if you can cook this good, you can knock down that wall." We were both laughing so hard…it was funny.

My son-in-law had to explain it to her. "Reagan is talking about God." I could tell by her expression she genuinely didn't get it. I'm hanging in there to do this symposium project, but Reagan believed he was put in office for a reason. I don't know if the committee will accept that."

Mrs. Noble unwaveringly replied,

"Just keep the idea working in the back of your mind… and, enjoy!"

I had no idea how I was going to explain the direction I was taking this project to my sponsor. Would he laugh if I explained God's providence ended the Cold War? Would he lose interest in sponsoring me? Hesitant to bluntly tell him, I chose to feel his reaction as I tried to explain, "Reagan was different from most other politicians. In other words, he didn't fit the political profile…he was a visionary, believing in something."

Dr. Yarborough suggested, "It has to contribute something, a theory that has been proven more than once that contributes to a new theory worthy of further research." I certainly didn't want this presentation to sound analytical – it would take the heart and meaning totally out of it. Discouraged as I pondered in thought of his suggestion, he grinned: "I can't wait to see what you come up with."

An hour later, I left the campus library, strolling along the sidewalk. Glancing over at the provost office…there I suddenly saw my sponsor striding up the stairs [leaping over a step in-between]…and Mrs. Noble frantically running up the stairs on the other side [racing to keep up with him] putting on her reading glasses as if she was headed for a serious confrontation! Doors flew open simultaneously on each side of the provost office as they rushed inside.

Puzzled by this adventurous scene, I thought: "What was *that* all about? Some coincidence…sponsor and co-sponsor who hadn't met one another, to my knowledge, rushing into the provost together. Could this have something to do with my research?

Only one other professor had a copy of this rough draft. Dr. Yarborough, waiting to see what I come up with, didn't even have a copy. Was someone vindictively attempting to abort this project? Oh well…what can they say when you find God in the archives?"

Intuitively fitting this puzzle together, it took me awhile to catch on. Cold War, nuclear missiles, Star Wars, and the Berlin Wall… God only knew what they must've been thinking! I made another appointment to discuss this with Mrs. Noble inquiring if we could salvage this research.

Mrs. Noble didn't disclose details, and I'll never know what conversations took place in the provost that day. Mrs. Noble confirmed, "We need to explain to the provost, on a level in which they can understand just what it is you're trying to do."

Analytical thinkers have a different thought process that often contrasts with intuitive thinkers. All too often, they over analyze missing the whole point of one's intentions. I can only speculate the adversary, but it wasn't worth inquiring. *Note it wasn't anyone mentioned in this book. I knew Mrs. Noble was pulling in my favor.

I explained to Mrs. Noble,

"The Cold War is a very rough topic. However, this isn't about the Cold War itself – it's about the greatness in people."

Mrs. Noble confirmed,

"Well, tell them that. Put it in your paper just as you're telling me."

I also mentioned,

"Reagan wasn't analytical."

Mrs. Noble agreed,

"No, he wasn't analytical."

She previously asked me to find out if the presentation had to be analytical, or if it could be research/findings. I told her they would accept research/findings. Mrs. Noble was relieved. All she could say,

"Thank God it doesn't have to be analytical!"

I asked what she thought of the Star Wars topic, and she assured it would be my decision. I was hesitant, at first, to go with Star Wars, because I may get a lot of questions I wouldn't be able to answer.

I explained to Mrs. Noble, "It's about the men…not the missiles." Again, Mrs. Noble said, "Tell them that." We could work together because we were able to comfortably communicate on the same page. Mrs. Noble didn't analytically judge what I thought – she knew how I thought.

Again, I wrote a narrative rough draft describing Ronald Reagan as a Hollywood Cowboy Rides into the Oval Office. This idea came from another's advice throwing it on a side-path. However, it was fun creatively describing how Reagan challenged the Soviets to a dual with nuclear missiles, how he threw his cabinet members into a tail-spin with his innovative idea of Star Wars, and how the analysts scoffed at Star Wars.

Once the analysts saw that Reagan wasn't going to give in…they all fell in line, including Voice of America and Radio Free Europe. President Reagan was a man of God, had providence on his side…oh well…if you can't beat 'em – join 'em. (Bannon).

This is where Gorbachev comes in; although, these two men couldn't come to an agreement [on eliminating nuclear missiles]

President Reagan commented to Gorbachev, "And you brought me all the way here for this!" (Gorbachev Memoirs pp.419).

This essay was true to events, yet written in a creative and fun style. It stirred up a misunderstanding again of what I was trying to do. However, once my sponsor's supervisor read this essay, an extended silence left me in suspense while I was sitting in his office.

Gathering his thoughts, he cleared his throat, "I just can't believe President Reagan bluffed Gorbachev with Star Wars!"

That wasn't my intent – that wasn't what I was saying. If this was a misunderstanding that I was making fun of Ronald Reagan – that was the farthest from the truth. I explained that my research question was did Star Wars end the Cold War? My point was the character and values of the men ended the Cold War more than the innovative idea.

He was convinced most historians would disagree. However, historians focus on the causes and effects of events. Other theories see the greatness in people, changing the course of history, making a difference in the outcome.

I touched base again with Mrs. Noble.

"Got a little problem, my sponsor's supervisor suggests most historians would disagree with my thesis statement. However, if I can prove my thesis I can present it in the symposium."

Mrs. Noble replied, "Could you send me the thesis statement and I'll talk to him and see what the problem was." Several hours later she asked: "Well…do you have substantial proof?"

Mrs. Noble had copies of all my research. What kind of a question was this?

I wittingly replied,

"Naw…I'm just making this stuff up as I go."

Apparently, this didn't come across with the tone as it would have verbally. After a couple days, no response, I apologized if I offended her. It's just that I've worked so hard on this research and the proof is right there in the archived dialogue.

Mrs. Noble assured,

"No, no you're fine! No offense taken. Did Star Wars really end the Cold War? OR, did it begin a dialogue between two men whose character (and values) ultimately – ended the Cold War?"

She was trying to help me with reinventing the statement giving Star Wars some credibility while maintaining my thesis statement. I visited her again in her office while she reviewed my essay. Mrs. Noble suggested, "Try not to be so creative." Making close eye-contact: "I want you to do this as a speech – like the one you did in my class."

Speech is the foundation I achieved under Gloria Noble's instruction making it possible to present this research in the 2012 Undergraduate Research Symposium. Dr. Yarborough formally agreed to sponsor me. He was intrigued by the essay.

Mrs. Noble replied,

"Great! Things are finally coming together for you."

I promised her I'd work over Christmas break to format this into a speech presentation.

Mrs. Noble and I shared a lively, adventurous year together on this research project. There was one other project we did this same semester. I had an opportunity to interview Gloria Noble. I'm thankful I saved a recording of her interview. I would all too soon discover Mrs. Noble would take a detour – a road less traveled by.

CHAPTER 5

The Interview

A Road Less Traveled

ONE DECISION CAN HAVE A profound effect leading to a chain of events. In other words, if I had continued as a business major, Mrs. Noble's path and mine may have gone separate ways. It would have been highly unlikely I would have had the opportunity to interview Mrs. Noble because this was my project from a writing class I would not have taken as a business student.

Changing my major to rhetoric writing made it possible for Mrs. Noble, and I to continue paths. September 2011, one year after being in her speech class, I was assigned to interview someone for a biography essay.

I chose Mrs. Noble because she encouraged me to pursue my degree in writing. Journalism was my desired goal…I had no idea Mrs.

Noble was a former journalism professor. She was eager to reveal her background through this interview…but there was something more – she revealed a connection, a path connecting to a purpose. Have you ever met someone and wondered why you met that person? Then later you are able to fit the pieces of the puzzle together? Coincidences don't just happen; especially, when one decision leads toward a series of connecting events. I cannot overemphasize had I stayed in business administration – this interview would have never taken place.

Mrs. Noble was eager to tell her story. Asking her if she'd agree to an interview, she optimistically replied, "Sure! When?" I had to gather the guidelines from my writing professor, make a list of five questions I sent Mrs. Noble to review prior to the interview.

Mrs. Noble had the listening role as a speech professor. She was an aspired reporter/journalist, so the interview was relatively simple… she did most the talking. I listened intently, took the back seat as the interviewer, as her story unfolded. I could tell she really enjoyed sharing her background. I could visualize her as this reporter/journalist, taking a detour to her path in teaching, rather than seeking a story – Gloria Noble became the story.

My questions focused on speech methods, but Mrs. Noble voluntarily revealed her days as a journalism professor. The university was only a two-year college, at the time, and she wasn't graduating enough students. She sent her students to pursue their internships – they were hired before they graduated!

Mrs. Noble read my questions for the interview and commented: "I had to laugh when I read this. Most students think I've been teaching speech all my life, and they really don't know my background. So, as I was reading this I had to think [with a sigh] she doesn't know my background." This told me she desired her background to be made known.

After all, in spite of her busy schedule, she went to the trouble to pull out her Autobiographical Sketch she wrote for admission into the doctorate program. Mrs. Noble was teaching speech full-time, preparing the course work for her classes, grading presentations, oh and she promptly answered student's e-mail questions…she was actively pursuing her doctorate and researching communications. I consider it an honor and privilege giving me her valuable time for this interview.

Mrs. Noble emphasized, "That's why I pulled this document out for you. I think when you read this document – you'll have a whole different perspective of Mrs. Noble. So, why don't you take that home and read it, and if you have any questions you can get back to me on it later." At that point, we began with the interview about her as a speech professor.

I was interested in her major achievement in her career. She described it as rolling and continuously ongoing without regard to any one major achievement. She had started in one discipline teaching journalism at the junior high and high school levels. Mrs. Noble emphasized, "I was going to be a reporter – I was going to be a journalist.

When I graduated they told me I needed to get some practice with interviews. There was an opening, in the Fort Smith public school system. I started teaching and…I was hooked. Never did I think I'd be teaching. Never did I think I'd even be in education at all especially, higher education."

She was very content where she was with her career. Mrs. Noble's colleague persistently calling her to come to the university, ignoring his calls, she humorously bargained: "I'll come by and apply if you'll promise me you'll quit calling." Thanks to her colleague's determination, in 1991, Mrs. Noble began teaching at Ridge Ford University.

That very same year, I began taking my nursing prerequisites. Looking back, I would have loved to have been one of her journalism students.

However, if I had my choice of knowing her then, or knowing her during her last two and a half years – I'd pick now over then. God gives multiple talents, but you can only travel one road at a time. I'll never know where the road would've led if I had been her journalism student, I wouldn't have been a nurse had I chosen a different path. More important, life is about fulfilling God's plans – in due season.

Nursing was that due season then. Taking care of people over the years is a very enriching experience. A service to those in need is a service to God. Maybe now the reward will come through another talent – to write – and be of service to Him in this area. Writing was always my desired dream and Gloria Noble was the mentor who inspired me to pursue my dream in writing. My enthusiasm accelerated to fulfill this dream knowing she had utmost confidence in my potential. Gloria confirmed that writing is what God intended me to do.

In nursing I had achieved my goal – in writing I am pursing my potential. God always puts the right people in the right place at the right time.

Gloria Noble emphasized: "My Intended Path Was Never – The Path I Ended Up On. Never did I dream I'd be working on my doctorate; especially after fifty. That's the next article I'm going to write – "Surviving College after Fifty." Mrs. Noble sighs: "Although, I haven't survived it yet." Through her optimistic laughter she added: "So…I laugh. I'm doing what after fifty?!" A brief silence filled her office…and again she reminds: "I'll let you read the document and you'll see what I'm talking about."

She took the lead doing most the talking and read aloud the questions I had on the paper. I think she did this as a favor to me because she probably sensed my apprehension as the interviewer. A brief silence gave me the opportunity to jump in and ask, "Have you ever had a student terrified…" Mrs. Noble: "I have." I continued: "…of public speaking?"

She repeated: "I have. That's why I give that PRCA [personal reference communication apprehension] test at the beginning of each semester. That gives me a clue of who I have in my class who has an extremely high level of apprehension. I can watch those students very closely. They don't know I'm doing this, and I don't want them to know. So…if I have one of those students not coming to class – they'll get an e-mail from me. 'Hey, I noticed you weren't in class. Are you coming back to class? Missed – ya!'

Some students think 'I'm not coming to class – she'll never know I wasn't there.' Well, yes I do know [laughter.] It's that little extra touch that students need."

The extra touch – of encouragement were three phrases that inspired me with the enthusiasm in pursing writing. Each phrase, just three-words, "Hang In There." "Go For It!" and "Just Go Girl!" That little extra touch demonstrates words are powerful, but it's the person's integrity that is more powerful.

Mrs. Noble had both credibility and integrity. She was very directive in teaching how to compose a speech. In her class, she complemented me for example: "Perfect, wouldn't change a thing." I wondered if she said this to everyone. However, when I ventured out into research – I had to write several drafts to meet her expectations.

Sometimes it got frustrating, but she'd always remind me to 'hang in there.' This experience clarified her integrity. In other words, I believe she would have been honest if I should have stayed in business administration. Anytime doubt crosses my mind, I think of Mrs. Noble's credibility. If I doubtfully question my potential – I would be undermining her credibility. So that's one motivational factor that a part of her continues to live on through my persistence.

Mrs. Noble recapped her thoughts toward my question about her major achievement. She added: "Surviving the changes in education over the last thirty years…I would say that's a major achievement. Working on my doctorate is also a major achievement. You see there are young professors coming in straight out of college with their doctorate degrees. I have all this experience, and there's so much I can't do without that degree." A crack in my voice expressed sensitivity: "But the experience helps too." Mrs. Noble somewhat agreed: "I'd really like to think so…yes."

One accomplishment Gloria Noble made during her last year was the opportunity to co-sponsor me in the 2012 Undergraduate

Research Symposium. She didn't have a category, but she could co-sponsor.

All the professors with categories had doctorate degrees and…no one co-sponsored in any other presentations – except Gloria Noble. It was a privilege for her to come aboard as co-sponsor and an honor for me to have her as my co-sponsor.

The symposium wasn't as significant as the working relationship we had. However, it was significant, and important to me, for her to be recognized as co-sponsor. We worked close on the Cold War project and she gave me a lot of encouragement. I know I wouldn't have "hung in there" had it not been for her. In essence it was my gift to her…and it was also her gift to me. I was Gloria Noble's speech student presenting a project that began in her speech class.

Mrs. Noble was always trying new methods that would reduce speech anxiety. For example, she started having the students work in teams of two during the introductory speech. Rather than talking about themselves – they would introduce each other. The introductory speech is where most students experience the highest apprehension level.

I asked, "We all have days that get off to a bad start. Is there anything you'd recommend before giving a speech when having one of those days?" Mrs. Noble added, "Uh um, talk to yourself, I know that sounds crazy. What I do is I go to my happy place. I spend five minutes with self-talk; especially, when I'm not having a good day. Actually, I'm having one of those days today." She never specified what was on her mind or why she wasn't having a good day.

Reflecting back on highlights of fun and memorable days Mrs. Noble wrote a book titled: *What Do I Write in my Journal?* It was about humorous experiences from students she had known. Mrs. Noble described some stories as "Ha hah funny." Other stories were, "'Are you kidding me?' type of funny." Her book is reader-friendly, a page turner that will keep you laughing at the thought Gloria Noble with her serious profile caught in these situations.

I asked her, "What do you write in your journal?"

She added, "For me, I'm really big into photography. I like a picture of the sunset because it's soothing, that's what keeps me calm."

Wrapping up the interview, again she mentioned, "You take this document home and read it. If you have any questions get back to me later." I was so impressed in hearing about her years teaching journalism I made it a point in closing, "I'd like to hear more about your days in journalism." Mrs. Noble responded in a winding down tone, "Yeah…well. That was an experience." I could sense she really missed teaching journalism.

Looking back I believe I had missed some significant points she was stating in the interview. The answers were in her autobiography sketch. One line that really caught my eye was Mrs. Noble quoted Frost: *A Road Less Traveled By.*

Gloria Noble had a missing piece in her life that would've been if only she'd taken the path of her dreams. Gloria Noble a reporter/ journalist, a missed opportunity in her life, a challenge in her life she never achieved. I remembered trying to get a primary source to interview and got a response from Mike Duggan from the Reagan Foundation July 18, 2011.

I didn't return his call because I was trying to get the university to invite a guest speaker and unable to find the right person to talk to whom could have accomplished this. I told Mrs. Noble maybe "we" could get an interview.

However, she wanted me to make the contact and conduct the interview. Truth is I wanted this interview to be her chance as a reporter/journalist. In other words, I was trying to fill her bucket-list before I was aware she had cancer. Mrs. Noble responded: "Let's talk – Come by sometime."

Wondering what on earth did she want to talk about? She looked like she wanted to say something. After a brief silence, and serious expression, guess she noticed how her optimism reflected toward me. Mrs. Noble seemed to avoid something she may have wanted to say, she opened the conversation.

We talked more in detail about the project. She gave direction on the thesis and forming a research question. Mrs. Noble making close eye-contact: "We're not going to read from the paper are we?" Both of us slowing shaking our heads: "I want you to do this as a speech like the one you did in my class."

I had a deep gut feeling there was something personal Mrs. Noble intended to share, yet didn't confront her. Second-guessing, thinking, "If it was that important, she would volunteer the information that is if she had anything to say. I may have read too much into her e-mail." There are still unanswered questions, but can't help but think gut feelings may be the most accurate. Gloria very likely concealed any personal information in order to maintain a positive influence. This would be her last project, and the first to co-sponsor. I think she knew that.

Unfortunately, we never conducted the interview. I learned more from her direction in forty-five minutes in her office than in any given semester. I truly hoped someday to have the opportunity to collaborate with her as a writer. There was just so much more I wanted to learn from her. I'm glad we had the opportunity to work close together on the Cold War project.

God put Gloria on my path to clearly define God's purpose for me, but he also put me on her path, at this point and time, for a purpose too.

Time is a fragile gift, and for her, the final chapter in her life would soon come to a close.

I had no idea this would be my first interview with her and...the last.

CHAPTER 6

A Serendipitous Path

I NTENDED PATHS – AN ESSAY from her interview was based on how journalism thrived in her speech class through the speech writing process. Intended Paths, was very lively, and upbeat reflecting Mrs. Noble's serious high-professional profile, yet revealing her sense of humor based on her book *What Do I Write in my Journal*? Overall, comparing my impression of Mrs. Noble in a real-life scenario was an analogy to the movie *"Mr. Holland's Opus."*

She impressively admitted, "Wow you did a good job! Not for sure I would want it published." I quickly apologized, if it gave her the wrong impression, if the humor was unsophisticated, if it undermined her professionalism – it wasn't my intent. Actually, this essay was highly complementary of Mrs. Noble.

A professor whose significance was through her encouragement and success of her students revealing that path intended.

"The path I intended was… never the path I ended up on." The essay focused on her taking a detour to teaching. However, there was an unforeseen path she did not reveal at the time. Mrs. Noble assured, "It has nothing to do with your wonderful article, but there are external factors that aren't positive, encouraging or motivating." I didn't probe into details, because I figured it may have had something to do with the journalism program closing.

Probing into her autobiographical sketch I noticed a revealing roadmap. A roadmap that connected what I wrote in December 2010 [unexpected detours] and what she wrote May 2009 [a road less traveled.] This was a crossroads where our paths significantly connected. When intended paths become unexpected detours there is a road less traveled by.

Later, from her interview, it became clearer to me – "I haven't survived it yet," and why wasn't she having a good day? Did a calming soothing sunset have any significance? For example, was her life entering into a sunset phase? Furthermore, in her autobiographical sketch, she closes with "There is no doubt that I have taken 'the road less traveled by,' and it has made all the difference. And I hope, as Frost said in his poem, 'Stopping by Woods on a Snowy Evening, that I have 'miles to go before I sleep.'"

Intended paths – Unexpected detours, her intended path was never the path she ended up on. In January 2012, I was taking my Symposium project through an editing class and asked Mrs. Noble to put in a good word for me. Mrs. Noble's path took an unexpected detour with cancer. My path would take an unexpected detour – fighting adversity.

Gloria Noble responded,

> "Dear Priscilla – I'm out this semester on medical
> leave. Currently I'm in Houston for treatment and will
> not be back for some time – sorry."

I mentioned I would keep her in my prayers. Things will certainly get better. I didn't feel right presenting in the symposium in her absence. She assured whichever timing I preferred would be fine. I decided on next year hoping she'd be back.

Mrs. Noble confirmed, "Okay, that's what we will do then. Here's to hoping all goes well!"

I was growing concerned about her response – "Here's to hoping all goes well!" Inquiring further I apologized if it was too personal to question how she was doing.

Mrs. Noble: "Priscilla – not too personal – I'm just trying to recover in the hospital. I have cancer – your prayers are welcome. Thanks."

The news that Gloria Noble had cancer was ultimately devastating! Mrs. Noble having cancer was certainly nothing positive, motivating or encouraging. I didn't question – I prayed!

I kept in touch with her weekly to see how she was doing. I didn't look back, at the time, to piece this puzzle together. The entire year of 2012 was a year to keep Mrs. Noble ceaselessly in my prayers.

I cannot say for certain, but speculatively reflecting back, I wonder if she knew she had cancer during the interview? In other words, was she trying to tell me something back then and I just didn't read into it close enough?

Shortly after the interview, I explained to her, "I'm sorry I didn't see the whole picture. The essay has reached its' intended audience – you."

However, the picture I focused on was the journalism program dissolving. I had no idea it may have been something more critical. A few months after Mrs. Noble told me she had cancer I assured her: "A writer's unpublished work is the most treasured." The unpublished biography will always be my most valuable article I will ever write.

CHAPTER 7

Fighting Two Battles

THERE'S ANOTHER ROAD LESS TRAVELED by… the side-paths, recognizing the people God puts on your path in the midst of adversity. Mrs. Noble apologized for not being able to be more help. I assured her there was no need to apologize – I wouldn't have come this far had it not been for her. She was the only one who encouraged me, co-sponsored, and stood by my side when no one else seemed to take this project seriously.

Mrs. Noble was in a Cold War fighting her battle with cancer while I was in a battle to get the Cold War project into the symposium. I encouraged Mrs. Noble to hang in there and I'll keep her in my prayers. Mrs. Noble: "Thanks Priscilla – just tell Angela we have been working together and that I said hello."

Dr. Angela Prescott, my editing professor, responded: "She is a really special person. I have enjoyed being her colleague. You know, you might be able to use that project as one of the assignments in our class."

Rendezvous at Reykjavik began as a five-page action-packed fun essay about Ronald Reagan, a Hollywood cowboy rides into the oval office, comes up with an innovative idea of Star Wars. It contained some comical dialogue between Reagan and Gorbachev yet maintained the seriousness of the Cold War. It was at Reykjavik, a summit held in 1986, where President Reagan and General Secretary Gorbachev misunderstood each other's intentions. Reagan was a former pacifist and… Gorbachev was a secret believer in God. (Anderson, 95 and Reagan, M. 207). In editing class, I worked on upgrading the paper into a formal format suitable for the undergraduate research symposium.

Mrs. Noble believed it was important to have fun with a project. I believe that is why she could see its' potential in the early stages. Mrs. Noble knew from my initial speech, about Ronald Reagan I presented in her class, I believed in his character and took this project seriously.

The initial shock to hear she was diagnosed with cancer I asked her if there was anything I could do or anything she needed. Did they find it at the early stages? She did not give any details – only thanked me and said, "Your prayers are welcome."

I reflected back on my criteria paper, that I wrote to Mrs. Noble end of the semester in her speech class. Intending to give words of encouragement and hoping she would respond I replied, "It's commonly taught we are where we are because of our choices – I beg to differ.

It certainly doesn't answer the question why bad things happen to good people. This is not anything you have chosen. I just can't fathom why *God* would allow this to happen to you. You have so much significance and purpose in life."

Mrs. Noble clarified, "Priscilla, I am currently in a battle for my life – literally and so am spending all my energies on such. Best wishes."

I could only glare at the e-mail. Could this be her way of brushing me aside by providing a protective environment? Did I say the wrong thing? My intentions were I truly cared about her.

The symposium project wasn't the primary importance. Gloria Noble was more than a professor – she was a mentor and friend. I understood she was in a battle for her life literally. Determined not to take her reply too personal I refused to take her reply literally – I refused to give up on someone very special, one who has had such a profound impact on my life, at the same time I was immensely praying for hers.

I was not going to detour away from keeping in touch. A friend goes the distance in both good times and bad. Hoping to be that friend to her needs I wished I could've done more.

Mrs. Noble,

"Do... whatever it takes to fight this. I know it's difficult to be positive, but as long as there's life there's hope. Meanwhile, depend on God to get you through this, and whatever means He provides. I've been praying like I've never prayed before. I trust you'll do the same. If you ever need a friend to talk to – I'll be there. I'm not great at keeping a conversation afloat but I am a good listener. I'm hoping your words intended to encourage me will be a blessing for you."

G.N. "Priscilla – Thank you for your kind words. If all goes well I might be back in the fall. Thanks again."

Mrs. Noble was a challenge-seeker, a challenge conqueror. I became vulnerable expressing my weak area questioning God – questioning why, why this, why now and...why Mrs. Noble? I think she sensed that.

I needed to remain strong to encourage her. Mrs. Noble was a fighter – a go-getter. She showed that characteristic in her journalism days, as a speech professor, and now she was determined to fight this battle with cancer.

Ultimately in my weakness, I found strength and courage to fight back. My unexpected detours encountered moments of adversity. It was easier getting the research from the archives than it was to obtain the guidelines required for the symposium. My sponsor kept directing me to his supervisor who sent me back to my sponsor.

My sponsor's supervisor suggested for me not to ask my political professor to sponsor me. I speculated – did Dr. Yarborough not wish to sponsor and didn't want to tell me, or was this his supervisor's idea? I was uncertain, so I e-mailed my sponsor, Dr. Yarborough, to clarify if he was still interested in sponsoring this project.

Waiting on a reply, his supervisor suggested reading twelve pages of research paper and insisted it was the guidelines. His criteria infused a heated argument. I replied, "It is unfeasible to read twelve pages in ten-minutes. I researched the running time – two minutes per page. By the way, I have an opportunity for an interview from Mike Duggan and may just wait 'til next year." He responded, "I think that would be a good idea to wait 'til next year."

However, I was not about to put this off. Mrs. Noble was in a battle for her life. Another year may be too late.

I knew I had to move fast – if she would be named as co-sponsor, and…I wasn't about to back down. I sent another reply to my sponsor's supervisor.

"Allow me to explain a few things. Speech was the most dreaded class I signed up. For five minutes I could get through a speech knowing somebody who believed in me was listening.

Mrs. Noble is my co-sponsor who has taken time out of her busy schedule to help me with this project. The plan was to present it the way she taught, looking at the audience – no reading from the paper. This project originated from a speech I did in her class."

He recommended for Mrs. Noble to sponsor me and present this as a speech project and not a research project. Again, Mrs. Noble did not have a category; therefore, she could not sponsor. Second, she was on medical leave and physically unable to be there.

He did refer me to the coordinator of the undergraduate research symposium who took immediate interest in my project. He agreed to credit Gloria Noble as the co-sponsor. I would need to seek a sponsor.

Mrs. Noble was in no position, in her situation, to know the adversity I was encountering. I never mentioned it to her.

Instead, I went to Dr. Prescott explaining it was suggested to abandon this as a research project and only do a speech presentation. Dr. Prescott was determined not to abandon it as research, with all the work invested in it, picked up the phone and called the provost office. Dr. Prescott smiling, while on the phone, asked the person in the provost office: "I'm calling to find out when Mrs. Noble will be back from medical leave?" I thought, "Uh oh…she doesn't know!

What will she think? I'm only a student and she may be offended if she found out a student knew about Mrs. Noble having cancer and Dr. Prescott [her colleague] not aware." Dr. Prescott was informed she would be on leave the entire semester and that's all they told her.

I rushed out of her office, ran down the hall, swung the door open, and just outside around the corner, ran into Dr. Yarborough who confirmed: "I just sent you an e-mail. Did you get it? Yes, I will be happy to sponsor you." I quickly thanked him, in a hurry to get to the library and e-mail Mrs. Noble. God pulls things together through the storm of adversity.

For example, I was told not to ask my professor to sponsor me. Unsure if he would, I again asked if he'd be interested. Meanwhile, the coordinator, interested in the research, confirmed I must find a sponsor. However, it all worked out. Again, God puts the right people in the right place at the right time.

I quickly e-mailed Mrs. Noble. "Dr. Prescott called the provost office inquiring when you're expected to return. I told her you were on medical leave put didn't give her the details. I don't think she knows. I kept the information between us confidential because I didn't feel it was my place to tell her. She really needs to hear this from you."

However, it was uncertain if Mrs. Noble would contact Dr. Prescott. I felt the urgency for these two professors to correspond. After all, Dr. Prescott thought well of Mrs. Noble and they were close colleagues.

Attempting to get the two together, I e-mailed Dr. Prescott: "I really think it's urgent you contact Mrs. Noble." This way, if one didn't make the contact – the other one would. It would be up to Mrs. Noble to decide whether or not to tell her.

Early in the semester when Mrs. Noble told me she had cancer, I wasn't in the mood to write let alone edit. Dr. Prescott stayed close to me and warmed up with a sincere understanding. She knew Mrs. Noble and I worked close together on this research project and developed a close working relationship.

The week in attempting to get the two professors to make contact, Dr. Prescott entered the classroom. It was evident she'd been crying, wiping away the remaining tears, she stepped up behind the podium. "If anyone is finding it difficult to write, let me ask – have you encountered any train wrecks lately?"

I took her reaction as if – yes she received the news. Yes, this was an emotional train wreck experience, a detrimental disaster. I cannot say what it was like for Mrs. Noble to struggle with cancer. She was my mentor and friend, now like a train hanging off the tracks, a detoured path.

I wanted so much to do something, yet felt helpless. However, to hear a professor has cancer is devastating to other professors and close colleagues – it can have a devastating impact on a student too.

Dr. Prescott suggested writing about our train wrecks, express our feelings and pour out all heart and soul onto paper. I wrote about how Gloria Noble's intended path was never the path she ended up on. Her and her paths – dog-gone path! I didn't turn in this paper to protect confidentiality. However, in another paper she wanted to know our writing interests. I did mention Mrs. Noble was going through a difficult time.

My writing profile consists of four words – to impact, inspire, persuade, and to make a difference. It must glorify God expressing life's meaning and true stories about real people, real experiences. For example, live each day as if it were your last, treat others as if it were their last; meanwhile, pursue a vision as if you were to live a hundred years.

Never did I dream when I wrote those lines I'd be writing this book about Gloria Noble. Mrs. Noble's character fits a mirror image of my writing profile. She has had a profound impact upon my life, she has inspired and persuaded me to become a writer, and encouraging me in public speaking – she has made all the difference.

Throughout the semester, Dr. Prescott remained close. She encouraged me to continue with my research project, gave me her time in her office to discuss not only this project, but also my writing career.

In the classroom, we moved the chairs in a wide-circle handing our papers to the student on our right while we edited a few minutes repeating this process. This way, when we got our papers back, at least three other students had edited, reviewed, and jotted suggestive notes. Dr. Prescott stayed close sitting just behind me. I could tell she knew I had carried a heartfelt heaviness that weighted down the ability to focus. There were times I wanted to run into Dr. Prescott's office and burst out: "Is she going to die?!"

I'm certain she knew Mrs. Noble was fighting cancer. I don't know if Dr. Prescott was aware how much I knew so, I guess that's why I never confronted her. It was as if we both wondered if the other knew, yet somehow sensed the other did. Dr. Prescott being silently supportive toward me never initiated the conversation, maybe I should have. I only wished we had conversed openly, because it would have helped to share those feelings with her since she was her colleague who was close to her too.

Most people feel uncomfortable talking about death or the possibility of death. Such an inevitable topic ought to be discussed openly. Mrs. Noble felt close enough to voluntarily share with me her personal fight with cancer. Dr. Prescott and I both maintained confidentiality thus creating a barrier to openly communicate.

However, she was a significant encouragement in Mrs. Noble's absence.

It was also significant I move on with this project. I needed to step up toward more formality with the essay. I didn't want to sound too analytical. It was important to let Reagan be Reagan to get the authenticity to the audience. Dr. Prescott agreed by writing "Yes!" commenting on my rough draft. I maintained the common dialogue for the first editing assignment about Hollywood Cowboy rides into the Oval Office and up-graded it to a formal research paper for the final project.

Time was running out and I needed to structure it into a speech format for the presentation.

Everything Mrs. Noble taught in her speech class served me well. Three is the magic number – think three most significant things. Get the message to the audience. Use clearly defined direction in where you are taking your audience.

I used the Reagan speech as a guideline. The three significant things about Reagan and Gorbachev both were – men of truth, neither desired a nuclear war, and both men believed in freedom.

I assured Mrs. Noble I was going ahead with the symposium this year because I wanted her to get the credit as my co-sponsor. She deserved this recognition because she stood behind me from the beginning, and it began in her class.

P.J. "Don't worry it will be a good one with a more serious straight-forward approach than my rough draft. I want the presentation to meet your approval."

G.N. "Sounds good. No worries."

This in turn told me Mrs. Noble had utmost confidence in me in moving forward with this project. Ideally, I wanted her to be here – I needed her here for direction. I understood she couldn't be present, but she was an e-mail away.

She lived to see this project succeed, her student succeed, and for her to have the opportunity to co-sponsor – I think she liked that. If I had waited another year for Gloria Noble to co-sponsor…it would have been a missed opportunity.

CHAPTER 8

The Symposium Experience

T HE WEEK THE ABSTRACT WAS due – it had to be revised. Without God in this, it would have been a missed opportunity. I was getting very discouraged telling God I have done all I know to do – least I tried. Ready to call it quits, I stopped in at Denny's to have supper. A lady sat in the booth in front of me. On the back of her t-shirt read "I know the plans I have for you declares the Lord – plans to give you hope and a good future" (Jer. 29:11 NIV). I considered this experience much like reading God's road-signs.

Eager to get home, I revised the abstract. The day the abstract was due for submission, my sponsor and I sat down together and did a third revision, not much changing only final touches. For example, Gorbachev was a secret believer.

Dr. Yarborough questioned the clarity: "A secret believer in what? One can be a secret believer in anything including Communism." I replied: "A secret believer in God."

Uncertain how he would respond, I was relieved when he confirmed: "Well…let's put God in there." God's hand moved in ending the Cold War and now God was moving in getting this presentation off the ground. We submitted the abstract one hour to the deadline!

Rendezvous at Reykjavik: A Look into the Character and Values of Ronald Reagan and Mikhail Gorbachev

Presented by Priscilla Jacobson

President Reagan ushers in a gigantic arms race with the Soviets, and then brainstorms an innovative idea to protect against a nuclear attack: The Strategic Defense Initiative (SDI) commonly known as Star Wars. The Reykjavik Summit reveals how these two leaders misperceived each other. Neither leader verified his beliefs. Ronald Reagan, a former pacifist, and Mikhail Gorbachev, a secret believer in God, came close to an agreement to completely eliminate nuclear weapons.

"Trust but Verify" became Reagan's motto when dealing with Gorbachev in future meetings. Star Wars often receives the most credibility in ending the Cold War. However, this paper argues that the character and values of these two leaders had the most impact in ending the Cold War.

If Star Wars existed in a previous era, it may not have had the same influence in ending the Cold War. Reagan's and Gorbachev's major achievement in ending the Cold War led to an intriguing research of the archives, Reagan's speeches, books from author who know Reagan and Gorbachev, and the viewing of original footage of Cold War events.

Evidence accumulated over the years has revealed that the character and values of both President Reagan and General Secretary Gorbachev had a major impact in ending the Cold War. The comparison of their character and values reveals that both of these leaders were men of truth, neither desired a nuclear war, and both men believed in freedom. More credit needs to go the men rather than the events in ending the Cold War.

Two weeks later, I sent Mrs. Noble the good news!

Dear Mrs. Noble,

"I received word that my abstract was selected for presentation. I understand it is important for you to get plenty of rest. However, since you are my co-sponsor, I want to include you in what I'm doing. So I'm sending you my power point and presentation outline. Check it over when it's convenient for you. Your input is important. Last picture, I did that for kicks… but I can delete that one. I'm keeping you in my prayers you'll hear good news soon."

Mrs. Noble responded, "Wow sounds great! Finally coming together for you! Congrats."

Mrs. Noble wasted no time in proof-reading my presentation. Two hours later she replied, "Hi, I would start with the attention getter and then go to the credibility statement, otherwise looks good."

She didn't comment on the last picture. It was Ronald Reagan and Mikhail Gorbachev both wearing cowboy hats. I chose to delete it, yet later discovered it would've come in handy during the presentation.

I was receiving the good news being selected to do my presentation in the 2012 Undergraduate Research Symposium. My only prayer was that Gloria Noble would receive good news about her battle with cancer. I continued to inquire if she heard any good news – no reply was indicating, no good news. All I could do is pray for her continuously.

Mrs. Noble could not be there for the presentation. However, she was on standby via e-mail giving me the direction and encouragement I needed.

After a year of extensive research and collaborating with Gloria Noble, the moment arrived – it was time.

Mrs. Noble,

"I'm mainly nervous about the question and answer session. Who knows what kind of questions they'll ask. I have the presentation practiced with speaker's notes, so I won't be reading from the paper."

We spent so much time together working on seeking the guidelines regarding research question and reviewing various ways to do the presentation. We never practiced the question/answer part. The only advice she could give on short notice: "You will be fine – just make sure you understand the question. If not, ask for clarification."

I figure she could tell staying connected with her by e-mail was my method of anxiety relief. Gloria Noble was not only my co-sponsor – she was my corresponding online coach. Returning her reply: "I know I'm probably overdressed, but hey they'll be thinking... 'That's one of Gloria Noble's students.'

I have you mentioned as co-sponsor in the presentation. I'll do the attention getter first and then go into the credibility statement as you suggested."

Mrs. Noble always stressed the importance to dress our best for our presentations in her class. Today, I dressed in the ultimate attire. I wore a white silk blouse with a formal black jacket with shiny black lapels, an academy award-style outfit with a bow layered over the lapel. I wanted Mrs. Noble to know I wanted to make a good impression for her as one of her students.

I know she was impressed when she commented: "Yay!!! Walk and breathe deeply."

Mrs. Noble,

"How have you been doing? Just wondering when you'll hear results on how things are progressing."

Only a couple of hours remaining and it'd be time. I'd be on in front of a live audience [of students, professors, colleagues, and a panel of judges] presenting in the 2012 Undergraduate Research Symposium, A Look into the Character of Ronald Reagan and Mikhail Gorbachev."

Mrs. Noble stated, "I start radiation and chemo on Monday. Good luck – I will be thinking of you!"

I will be thinking of you – the most uplifting comment just hours before my presentation. She couldn't be there physically, but she'd be thinking of me in her absence. I wished she could have been there to see it, but she had the outline, power point, and later I sent her a copy of the research paper. Knowing her thoughts were with me boosted my enthusiasm in my performance. Of course, I had last minute moments of nervousness with still an hour to wait.

Dr. Yarborough could not be there because he had an out of town conference. My former political professor, Dr. Brewer filled in to introduce me. I reminded him I prayed, aced his final exam…and now all I can do is – pray.

I felt as if I didn't belong here. Other presentations would be highly intellectual, analytical…and I'll be galloping in there with my political drama. Dr. Brewer reassured, "Don't worry – just remember you've researched and know more than they do." More important, I reminded myself God exalts common people to glorify him.

We quietly walked in and sat on the back row while the speaker was presenting just ahead of mine. Less than fifteen minutes and I'd be on. I quickly glanced inside Mrs. Noble's book *"What Do I Write in my Journal?"* Inside the front cover was Julie's card with the verse she gave me. Underneath Mrs. Noble's autograph I had a copy of her e-mail: "You'll do great – I'm sure of it."

No need to think what to put in my journal for encouragement – I take her book. Of course, I had my speaker's notes. However, Dr. Brewer didn't have any notes on what to say to introduce me. He asked if it'd be all right if he read my biography excerpt.

"Priscilla graduated from the LPN program at Ridge Ford Community College in 1995. She has been a nurse in long-term care for sixteen years. Priscilla is a returning student majoring in rhetoric/ writing with a minor in political science. She aspires to pursue a second profession in journalism.

Her research interests include political history, early American government, and presidential achievements. She loves researching the archives learning about the greatness in people. She is researching the Cold War and plans to research former presidents and also the leaders in Great Britain including Churchill, and Thatcher and their roles in the Cold War. Priscilla was my former student in American government and told me today she prayed and aced the final exam in my class. May I proudly introduce to you Priscilla Jacobson as she presents Rendezvous at Reykjavik – A Look into the Character and Values of Ronald Reagan and Mikhail Gorbachev.

I became extremely nervous when my sponsor's supervisor entered in and sat down, on the front row, beside Dr. Brewer who had just introduced me. After all, he understood I was going to wait 'til next year. He sat there with a big grin. My thoughts racing, "Oops got caught! Is he here to trap me in the question/answer session?"

Overwhelmed with feelings of intimidation, I briefly glanced over to Dr. Brewer sitting next to him. His eyebrows forged a worried expression. I quickly thought: "He hasn't seen my presentation. Surely he'll think, "What has her sponsor gotten me into?!" The cameraman stood over to my left mid-section in the audience patiently waiting. If I needed Mrs. Noble – I needed her here…now!

Focusing toward the back of the audience, I laid down my speaker's notes I had endlessly rehearsed. I already knew what I was going to say. I opened up with the attention-getter, as Mrs. Noble suggested, then moving on to the credibility emphasizing this project began in her class.

*Note: Appendix B includes the presentation

I saved the analysis for the last power point frame. I didn't want to have a lot of analytical verbiage on the power point. The main idea was to reveal who these men were, what they stood for, and what they believed in. The power point slides were photos that told the story along with the oral presentation. I used photos of Reagan announcing SDI, two photos of the Strategic Defense Initiative, the Reykjavik summit, the young Ronald Reagan in Hollywood, Crusade for Freedom and the Moscow speech under the bust of Lenin. I also used a couple of photos of Mikhail Gorbachev including portraits, fireside chat with Reagan, both signing the INF treaty, Reagan and Gorbachev standing at the Red Square. The last slide was explaining the research.

Thesis: The character and values of Ronald Reagan and Mikhail Gorbachev had a major impact in ending the Cold War.

Method: Archives, Reagan's speeches, eyewitness authors, original film footage of Cold War events.

Research Question: Did Star Wars end the Cold War?

Findings: It is highly unlikely Ronald Reagan, a former pacifist, and Mikhail Gorbachev, a secret believer in God would start a nuclear war.

Conclusion: The convictions of Ronald Reagan and Mikhail Gorbachev together ended the Cold War.

Contributing Factor: In spite of the chain of events – "It is the greatness in people who makes the outcome possible."

Opening the floor, inviting the audience to ask questions, a brief silence filled the room. Were they unsure what to ask, or were they concerned I'd be unsure what to say? Dr. Brewer was the first to inquire by raising his hand, "Would you say that Reagan and Gorbachev were friends?"

This was a simple question – the answer simple. I replied, "Things didn't get off to a good start, but yes I'd say they were friends." This would have been a prime opportunity to show the slide, I didn't save, of Reagan and Gorbachev both wearing cowboy hats. If I'd saved that photo, it may have gotten a few laughs, but it would've been difficult to convince the judge the question/answer session wasn't staged. Surprisingly, the questions were relatively simple. Once Dr. Brewer asked the first question, several hands in the audience raised.

"Would you say Reagan was a pacifist although he promoted the arms race?"

I explained: "I studied Reagan's forgiving character closely and how he valued human life. Deep-down I would say he still had those convictions, yes."

Only one man in the audience stirred up controversy, "I just don't get what you're driving at! Aren't there other things that ended the Cold War say the economy?" I wasn't intimidated with his remark because I knew there were a lot of supportive people in the audience attentive to my presentation.

I tactfully replied, "Well…yes, there were a lot of factors that ended the Cold War including the economy; however, the point I'm making is character and values is most important thing that stood out in ending the Cold War. To answer your question, this wasn't the first time the Soviet Union experienced a bad economy and the Cold War didn't end during previous economic decline."

The judge raised her hand and asked, "What did you learn from this research, and what can we learn from it today?"

With utmost confidence, I quickly gathered thoughts regarding the pertinent information. The judge's questions were the ones I needed to answer most significantly.

Making direct eye contact, I boldly replied: "The unique thing I learned is I had no idea Ronald Reagan was a former pacifist, or that Mikhail Gorbachev was a secret believer in God. Just think for a moment, a former pacifist and a secret believer competing in a gigantic arms race, yet missing an opportunity to eliminate nuclear weapons from the face of the earth – simply because neither disclosed his beliefs."

In answering the second-part of her question, recollecting my thoughts on the one source that provided the foundation that helped in formatting the presentation. Restating her question, "What can we learn from this today?

According to "Talking Points" from the Reagan Foundation archives, President Reagan sent a letter to Shevardnadze, giving a message to General Secretary Gorbachev, 'I want you to know who Ronald Reagan is, what he stands for, and what he believes in, and I expect the same from you.' Now voters must vote with those points in mind. In other words, it's vital to study the presidential candidate's character. After all Reagan once said: 'It is people who make America happen every day.'"

The judge slightly tilting her head nodding once as the corners of her mouth formed a kind of uhm expression. It was as if she was thinking, "Very impressive – I'm convinced." It was evident she was very pleased with my reply.

The audience acceptingly applauded. The first person to approach me shaking my hand was…my sponsor's supervisor!

He sincerely commented, "You did an excellent job!" Until this point I considered him an adversary. Anytime you do what God wants you to do, there will be adversity – expect it. Sometimes they need to see first-hand, people who have strong convictions – people who conquer challenges. Once your adversaries see that you are steadfast in your faith, they too will be convinced. It's important to forgive your adversaries because they're not only there to test your faith – but sometimes this reassures their faith.

Eager to send word to Mrs. Noble – I filled her in on the details about the presentation and the question/answer session including compliments. Again, reminding her, I couldn't thank her enough for co-sponsoring me and certainly couldn't have done this without her encouragement.

Mrs. Noble replied, "I am so happy for you!!"

Her character-trait, cheering on other people's success, is one I will always remember. I believe my persistence held strong in getting into this symposium because I did it for her too. She deserved a category yet, Mrs. Noble's opportunity to co-sponsor, and living to see her student succeed in a research project we worked so closely together on – I think she liked that.

I put together the formal research paper – twelve pages with footnotes on all the material relating to the presentation. I had a lot of sources to review. In my research class, learning to annotate, summarize, and include sources in my file was my saving grace.

It would've been impossible to remember exactly where all the sources belonged without pre-writing an annotated file. Even so, it was a tedious – time consuming effort putting this research paper together. Fortunately, I was permitted to use it for my next paper in editing class.

I experienced yet another adversary in editing class, not the professor – a student! I got my paper back…wasn't edited at all! It was full of remarks including: "God may have been a part of this but you act like God had everything to do with it!!!"

Included, in this formal research paper, the one on one conversation between Reagan and Gorbachev about "I'd like to fix my son a gourmet dinner, have him sit down and enjoy the meal, then ask him if he believed there was a cook." Gorbachev's reply: "The only answer possible is yes."

This was my favorite in the archives. It was more feasible to elaborate in more detail and clarity, in the research paper, compared to the time constraint of a ten-minute presentation. I explained to Dr. Prescott: "I cannot edit this paper according to this student's specifications.

First, I'd have to deny God. Second, I'd have to deny who these two leaders were, what they stood for, and what they believed in. Now I believe everyone has a right to his view, but he needed to learn editing ethics. I just wonder what Reagan would say?"

Recalling what Reagan said to the protesters at the Brandenburg Gate, and rephrasing his statement to fit the occasion: "If this is the type of editing that he so chooses to seek…I just wonder if he would have anything to edit again?!"

I refused to edit my paper, but to prove a significant point, I wrote to Dr. Prescott: "I'll edit this to one line…GOD…ENDED…. THE COLD WAR!" I wrote this bold statement only hours before the symposium results were posted.

Of course, the provost committee had already selected the top presentations. My point is, it's imperative to hold steadfast in your faith in God – HE will do the rest. Wednesday, April 25, 2012 at 4:28 p.m. a message from the Provost

Ms. Jacobson,

Thank you for your participation in the 5th Annual Undergraduate Research Symposium at Ridge Ford

University. The conference was a huge success, and all who participated are to be congratulated for showcasing the breadth and depth of knowledge here at our university. The symposium attendees enjoyed a wide variety of research projects representing all the academic colleges within the university, and our panel of judges had an incredibly difficult time selecting the best presented research projects of the day.

However, I am pleased to formally announce that the judges have selected your presentation, "A Look into the Character and Values of Ronald Reagan and Mikhail Gorbachev," as one of the top oral presentations at this year's symposium.

The provost forwarded this announcement to numerous professors – including Gloria Noble.

Mrs. Noble replied, "Wow, how exciting! Congrats to Priscilla – nice work! It was a pleasure to work with you." – Mrs. Noble.

The provost asked for me to submit a final draft of my research presentation for publication in the university's online anthology. I submitted the formal research paper to the provost – no changes made. I turned in this same paper in editing class…again, no changes.

Dr. Prescott graded on editing techniques and not writing. However, she handed my folder to me smiling: "I have a surprise for you."

Dr. Prescott put a grade on this unedited paper – 100%! She attached a note: "As the writer – you make the decisions." Again, God used her in a significant role in Mrs. Noble's absence. It was a pleasure to work with Dr. Prescott. Unfortunately, it was Dr. Prescott's last semester – she was retiring. I wished I had the opportunity to thank her.

CHAPTER 9

Staying In Touch

I took the opportunity staying in touch with Mrs. Noble during her final year. The research complete, the symposium presentation accomplished, yet I maintained contact simply because...I truly cared. Never did I think I would never see her again this side of eternity. Memories – good memories of someone so significant leaves a lasting impression of believing in God, and in one's self.

The research experience was a lively, adventurous project. For example, adventurous events of being misunderstood, hanging in there through adversity, and I'll never forget Gloria Noble and my sponsor racing up the stairs to the provost office – now that was a lively scene.

Furthermore, it all began in her speech class. Mrs. Noble's speech instruction made it possible for me to do the presentation. Otherwise, I would have had this research, but no confidence in presenting it before a live audience. In other words, the research would've been useless as symposium material had it not been for Mrs. Noble.

I wanted to thank Mrs. Noble for all she had done. I stayed in touch with her weekly concerned about how she was progressing. I only wished I could have done half as much as she did for me. Thanking her wasn't enough – I wanted to do more. Mrs. Noble was such an encouragement to me, so it was now my turn to be an encouragement to her.

2012 became a year for encouragement…and prayer. I really wanted to visit and regret never asking. It is possible to be overly polite waiting for an invitation. What kept me from paying Mrs. Noble a personal visit?

Fear – fear I'd be intruding. I knew Mrs. Noble spent countless hours with her students. Now was her time to spend with her family. I didn't know her family. Who was I to visit? After all…I was just a student. I know Mrs. Noble wouldn't have looked at it that way.

The only thing left to do was to stay in touch by e-mail to keep her uplifted, in hope of a positive outcome. There's only so many ways one can inquire about someone's doing. I was running out of words to say.

I asked if there was anything I can do. She never specified – only thanked me. I sent her a book titled *What Cancer Cannot Do*, and Max Lucado's book *In The Eye Of The Storm*. It didn't seem like enough, sending her a couple of books, and not being there for her. I kept her in my prayers hoping she would win this battle with cancer. I asked how things were progressing.

In May, Mrs. Noble replied,

"Hi, still in the middle of treatment 2."

She added it would be several months before she would hear any results. I encouraged her to hang in there, and mentioned I wanted to write a book about her. Mrs. Noble suggested, "We'll defer 'til fall."

She was hoping to return to teaching in the fall, and I was eager to see her recover. Back then, I had no idea she would be teaching online. Mrs. Noble never returned to campus.

In spite of her struggle hanging in there, while recovering from radiation, Mrs. Noble continued to encourage me to hang in there with my studies. I would soon keep her posted on how the semester was progressing while asking how she was doing. Mrs. Noble never clearly answered how she was doing…really. I was sure if she had good news to share she would tell me – no news isn't always good news.

I inquired by narrowing to more specific questions. "How are things going with your recovery? In other words, are chances good of it going into remission? I realize it's too early to know, but is the prognosis good?"

Mrs. Noble replied, "Only 30% of people with this type of cancer survive. I'm hopeful."

Inquiring further, "Did they say what stage it's in? In other words…is there a good chance you could be in the 30 percentile of the survivors?"

Mrs. Noble specified, "Stage 3 and they really don't know."

I remembered, in her classroom, the sign posted pointing to the waste basket that read, "Negative comments go here." Mrs. Noble always told me to hang in there. Likewise, I told her to hang in there. I did tell her I hope the words she used to encourage me will be a blessing for her.

"I'm hopeful" the key words telling me she was hanging onto hope. I wasn't about to take that hope away. All I knew to do was to follow her lead. Deep down, I felt she wasn't telling me everything; although, I wasn't for sure. I never could bring myself to ask her if she was going to die.

There was only one other person who I shared this unique roadmap writing experience. Mindy, a good friend of mine and co-worker, agreed this intertwining path was an experience from God in how He moves connecting certain people in our lives for a purpose. I shared with Mindy, "I really don't think she's telling me everything." Mindy made a point, "Do you go with your heart...or your head?"

I told her, "Of course, you go with what your heart tells you." Mindy shaking her head, "No...no that's not what I'm saying. You go with your head." In other words, patting her hand over her heart explained, "Your heart is telling you everything is going to be all right, but your head knows it really isn't. The reason Gloria isn't telling you everything is because she doesn't want to hurt you. She senses how close you feel to her – she doesn't want to worry you."

I remember how I worried about her when she told me she was having surgery in Houston. Worried about what kind of nurses took care of her. I'm sure she had good nurses. However, as a nurse, I know it's common to get caught up in the routine forgetting about the personal needs of the patient. It's the simple needs, often overlooked, from a glass of water, an extra pillow, to needing a nurse – who will listen. Gloria was on my mind and in my prayers while I took care of my patients.

I slowed down taking time with every patient. I couldn't be there for Mrs. Noble, so I took care of each one of my patients as if I were taking care of her. By day, I prayed her nurses would have empathy and be attentive. By night, I prayed angels would watch over her.

Meanwhile, I asked God for a miracle – that she would win this battle with cancer.

I assured her, "Long as God has a plan, and a purpose for your life here, and I believe He does, God will sustain you. People have had a belief system so strong that have defied odds, law of averages, and statistics. Reagan proved this by boldly stating: "Beliefs become realities." Hoping to give her the encouragement she had given me, Mrs. Noble continued fighting this battle throughout the year.

Well into the fall, Mrs. Noble replied, "Hi, I will be starting chemo again probably next week, still fighting the battle. Hang in there – stick close to your professors and talk to them often."

Still fighting the battle set an uplifting tone that Mrs. Noble was hanging in there and encouraged me to also hang in there with my writing. I focused so much on the emphasis to the first sentence – I failed to catch the significance of the second half. Stick close to your professors and talk to them often. What was she trying to tell me? Was this her way of subtly implying she wouldn't be around much longer?

Again, hanging in there in Non-Fiction Writing class, I was given the opportunity to write about the symposium experience titled Symposium and Serendipity. This time I added more insight from an enlightened spiritual appeal.

For example, Catholicism became a widely televised event during the end of the Cold War era which inspiring religions of the world pulling people of diversified faiths together in their fight against Communism. President Reagan and Pope John Paul shared a common interest in God. Both were survivors of assassination attempts. President Reagan maintained strong convictions that providence spared his life, and it was God's plan for him to end the Cold War. (Bannon.)

What this is really about are my Reykjavik moments getting into the Symposium. It all began in a speech class in 2010. Reagan came up with his innovative idea for Star Wars from a movie, and I came up with a great speech idea from the movie *The Reagan's.*

This speech focused on Ronald Reagan's character and values of his integrity, duty, and hope with excerpts of his speech from the 1976 convention where he addresses "two superpowers aiming nuclear missiles that could in a matter of minutes destroy the society in which we lived" (Reagan, R.W. 1976).

I watched *The Reagan's* numerous times and didn't buy into most of the researcher's analysis. Striving to get into the archives to no avail, I thumbed through Peggy Noonan's book When Character Was King. She mentions the Reykjavik deal – something Reagan wouldn't do because he didn't think it was right (Noonan 287).

I was puzzled in regard to her vagueness in explaining. I Googled what was the Reykjavik deal with Reagan? The computer bounced me into The Reykjavik File: Previously Secret U.S. and Soviet Documents from U.S. and Soviet Archive. Just like Reagan's Star Wars idea, this research was my serendipitous moment!

In spite of being informed, "You can't research a belief system – it won't work." Not many people believed Reagan's Star Wars idea would work (Bannon). My favorite dialogue from the archives is Reagan and Gorbachev's One on One meeting. President Reagan used imagery to make a point to prove God's existence with an analogy of enjoying a gourmet dinner then questioning if he believed there was a cook. Gorbachev's reply: "The only answer possible is yes" (The Reykjavik File). Yes, it is possible to research a belief. After all, how can anyone possibly argue when you find dialogue about God in the archives?

My experience in getting into the symposium was full of Reykjavik moments – misunderstandings and being misunderstood. Everyone had an analysis but no one had any answers. I encountered more difficulty getting information on the guidelines than I did in obtaining the research.

I kept getting contradicting opinions from too many people that included anything from doing an XY theory to entertaining the audience with Hollywood Cowboy Rides into the Oval Office…and finally, just read directly from a formal research paper.

That's easy for them to say if they hadn't studied Reagan's personable character. I knew from my research Ronald Reagan wasn't analytical. How can you analyze someone who isn't analytical? I wasn't going to do it because it just didn't seem right.

Gloria Noble co-sponsored this project. She encouraged me when other people didn't seem to take this research seriously. It was important to just let Reagan be Reagan if the authenticity of the message is going to reach the audience.

Mrs. Noble, "We're not going to read from the paper are we? I want you to do this as a speech – like the one you did in my class."

I presented this as a speech in the 2012 Undergraduate Research Symposium.

The judge asked, "What can we learn from this today?"

I responded, "Among the archives called Talking Points President Reagan sent a message to Gorbachev stating: "I want you to know who Ronald Reagan is, what he stands for, and what he believes in, and I expect the same from you" (Talking points). "Now if voters will vote with those same points in mind when choosing a candidate… maybe America will get back to what America ought to be." Ronald Reagan was a visionary but he looked back to the Founding Fathers and where America began.

Growing up I remember people talking about the Cold War. People feared a nuclear war was very possible. Looking back, I believe America had stronger religious values.

President Reagan didn't have analytical answers but based his decisions on his faith in God. Religions pulled together in spite of their differences. I believe the Cold War ended because, around the world, people prayed. If this research leads to greater opportunities – I'll always remember in a speech class is where it all began. Analysis doesn't have the answers to every situation…but prayer will assuredly get God's attention.

I sent a copy of this essay to Mrs. Noble. The last sentence was addressed directly talking to her. It was my way of saying God won't let her down. I don't know if she ever caught onto the significance of this message. Of course, I was hoping God would help her win her battle with cancer – He answers prayers, just not always in the way we desire.

Mrs. Noble replied,

"Well done. Thank you for sharing."

Her response, "Well done" told me she was very pleased with the religious significance. Reagan and Gorbachev didn't reveal their beliefs, yet God's hand moved in ending the Cold War.

God's hand moved in putting a professor and her student peacefully together in the midst of a Cold War project. Neither did we specify our beliefs. We need not beg to differ. God moved in this project every step of the way. Catholicism focuses on a vertical hierarchy while Protestants focus on a horizontal equality. The two working together...makes the sign of the cross, doesn't it?

Mrs. Noble and I came from opposite Christian backgrounds, yet [in essence] we accommodated one another's belief...without even knowing it. I thought highly of Mrs. Noble, and she treated me as an equal. This experience ought to shed some light on how Christians need to respect other Christian's views. Even when The Berlin Wall imposed a communication barrier,

President Reagan revealed when the light struck the television tower...it made the sign of the cross (Brandenburg Gate speech 1987). God profoundly reveals himself through otherwise missed opportunities. The vertical and horizontal roadmap meets at the center of the cross. Christ's character was able to shine through a professor and her student who saw the good in each other through unrevealed beliefs...just by letting God reveal himself in His own way.

CHAPTER 10

A Missed Opportunity

THERE IS BUT ONE THING I regret. I never visited her not once. Fear was another thing that kept me from not visiting; although, many times I wanted to visit. How would I react – what would I say? I wanted to sit down beside her and cry. I knew she wouldn't want that.

I sent her a Max Lucado study bible she received four days before her last Christmas. Mrs. Noble sent a reply: "Thank you for this beautiful gift." Why didn't I just take it to her? I recall her saying: "Stay close to your professors and talk to them often."

I missed the opportunity to ask: "What are you trying to tell me?" By this time, I was no longer overwhelmed that she had cancer. I became confident she would survive. I missed the opportunity when I should have drawn closer – I was unintentionally looking the other way.

It may have been God's way of providing that protective environment, preserving positive memories. In other words, it may not have been intended for me to see her in her last months, but to remember her when she was so full of life.

The last time I remember seeing Mrs. Noble, she was walking across the street to the campus parking lot. I was opening my car door and we happened to notice one another at a distance. An existing closeness thrives through the distance of time and eternity. I shared this missed opportunity with Mindy who assured, "You did the right thing, she'll always be in your heart…and now she's your angel."

I hope I have been half the influence and encouragement to her as she was to me – I'd like to think so.

All too often there's not enough time to say everything that ought to be shared. A bible is a wonderful gift of eternal value – you never know whose hands it will fall into or how it will inspire their lives.

2013 had been a difficult year, but recapping the criteria paper I did in Gloria's class had continued to serve its' purpose well. People choose their criteria based on their beliefs and values. The more I reflected on what I would have done different, the more I realized my friend Mindy was right in saying I did the right thing. I wanted to do more and – say less. If only I had known for certain Gloria's time would be short what would I have said? I made a list of criteria based on cause and effects of not knowing how short her time was against the criteria based on what I would have done different had she told me.

If only I had known, all the facts and outcome, I would have given sympathy, but not knowing gave hope. I really wanted the opportunity to share final words with her to take the road less traveled – it's the most important road. I'm sure she knew to do that.

I believe what I shared with Gloria – she knew I thought well of her. Not knowing she wouldn't survive, Gloria knew every word I said was authentic. However, if only I had known, rather than seeking another interview, I would have visited, this time – no questions, no recorders, and no notes. Rather than asking if there was anything I could do, I would have just done more and said less. I should have been closer, been there for her, than at an e-mail's distance.

Of course, as a Christian and a nurse, that would be my criteria. However, speculatively speaking, what would have been Gloria's criteria?

She was a professor – I was her student. Now for Gloria, an aspired reporter/journalist, she would probably believe authentic words have equal value as works. Different people are given different gifts. Actually, I was entering her territory of criteria and I think that's what she desired. May be that's one reason she didn't reveal how short her time would be.

She knew I was a nurse aspiring to become a writer. It could have been her way, and God's way, of keeping me on the path to fulfilling my potential, a gift for writing, that Gloria repeatedly confirmed. So, then again it may have not been such a missed opportunity.

CONCLUSION

I KEPT IN TOUCH WITH GLORIA Noble weekly. Sometimes she would answer e-mails right away…other times she wasn't feeling well and delayed her reply. She needed rest, so I tapered off to every other week.

Regretfully, I should have stayed in closer contact with her toward the end. The beginning of the year was so shocking to hear she had cancer. When fall arrived, I got used to the idea she was actively fighting her battle and confident she would survive.

The last e-mail from her was on January 14th advising me on the next project. I became so busy working on the project and never imagined her funeral would be precisely one month to the day…Valentine's Day. Deep down, I felt as if she wasn't telling me everything. I finally built the courage to ask her straight-forward if she would be in the thirty-percentile of the survivors. She taught on-line classes 'til her last days.

I noticed her name was dropped on the course list. I figured Mrs. Noble had taken a turn for the worst. I bought her a card about how Jesus walks with us through the rough paths in our lives.

Dear Mrs. Noble;

When intended paths lead to unexpected detours – The Road Less Traveled is the most important road. Until then, "Never – give up hope." No matter what the outcome, you are a significant mentor who has given me hope to never give up on my dreams. Meanwhile, I'll continue to pursue my potential in writing. Thank you for being more than a Professor, but also a friend. If I can do anything for you please let me know. Thinking of you and keeping you in my prayers always.

Love You;

Priscilla

I came so close to mailing the card, yet something deep-down urged me to wait until I checked my e-mail.

February 26th, 2013 I received an e-mail "This is Gloria's daughter. She passed February 8th." Excusing myself from class, unable to hold back the tears, a cameraman quietly stepped out of the library. Gloria included a message in her e-mails: "Life is not about weathering the storm, but it's about learning to dance in the rain." Her words intended to encourage me – I hoped would be a blessing for her...and they have. The card I didn't send...was intended for me – a reminder to continue pursing my potential fulfilling my dream.

It wasn't until after I read her obituary I discovered that Gloria is a Christian. I state this in the present-tense because she left this life as a Christian and today is with the Lord. Neither of us disclosed our personal beliefs. Some people consider it imperative to openly profess their faith while others believe in quietly reverencing God.

Either way, I learned through my research, God mysteriously moves by pulling people, of diversified faiths, peacefully together glorifying God through their character. God put a professor and a student together, in the midst of a Cold War project, just as He pulled people of diversified faiths together in their fight against Communism.

Gloria Noble gave up so much opportunity and could have been a reporter/journalist. To say she had reached her full potential, here on earth, would be an understatement. I'm surprised she wasn't a retired reporter/journalist teaching classes as a second profession. Gloria was multi-talented in giving direction. I could see her potential as supervising other reporter/journalists.

Taking the road less traveled by she implies there were no regrets because the road less traveled has made all the difference. However, if Gloria has ever looked back during the sunset of her life here and wondered if she'd do it the same as she did back then,rest assured, I'm confident the Lord has rewarded her with what she aspired to be, a reporter/ journalist. I can only imagine…Gloria… in Heaven, interviewing people – people I can only research. Yes – There is Life Out There.

As I reflect on memories – how will I remember Gloria Noble? I will always remember Gloria with her uplifting lively expression when I stated, "A song that would describe me is Reba McEntire's hit song *Is There Life Out There*?" A song not only describing me, but describes Gloria – a challenge seeker so full of life.

Whatever the reason, it was a lively scene, a sight to see, as she raced up the stairs along with my sponsor into the provost office. I'll remember how she hung in there with me believing in my potential.

Most of all, I'll never forget the intertwining path and how our writing correlated. I often wondered if she was thinking the same thing about this roadmap writing. I think she sensed this connection too. Not knowing how to approach her to share I picked up on this connection, I sent her an interview question.

"Describe some dancing in the rain experiences which had unexpected detours of good outcomes."

Mrs. Noble's comment: "You're fine – I got it!" I think she was letting me know we were both seeing the same thing. Ironically, the day of her funeral – it rained. A friend shared a belief, only few people are aware, rain at a funeral is a sign of blessings. My friend smiled, "Don't worry – Gloria went straight to Heaven that day."

When I feel I need her here – God has great plans for her up there. No, I cannot fathom why God would take Mrs. Noble who had so much significance, but I can only imagine the good eternal outcomes God has in store. Not only is she embraced in His glory, next time Gloria won't be sitting in the back above the audience. She'll be in Heaven making her way through the crowds to get a front-seat view as she cheers on her many students.

In the book of Hebrews it mentions a cloud of witnesses (Heb 12:1.NIV). Now that Gloria is living, in the presence of God, I'll remember her words just hours before the symposium, "You'll do fine – I'll be thinking of you." I'll never forget Gloria she was a God-send, like an angel by my side. I'll always remember…in her speech class is where it all began.

In The Garden of Prayer

2012 THE YEAR OF PRAYER – a prayer answered but not in the way desired. This I believe, when God takes someone away – he gives back so much more. Thinking memories are all that's left, but are they? There is a significant purpose in writing this book.

Through my story, I hope to influence professors to value their students. Professors are in a significant position to make a difference. I hope students who read this book will appreciate their professors. I certainly appreciated Gloria Noble. Professors have a tough job and… maybe you are a student who has a role of significance to inspire your professor making a difference in his/her life too.

Perhaps nurses will be inspired through this story and realize how vital their lives really are and the people they care for. Anyone in a battle to survive, rest assured – there is hope, both here and beyond. My hopes are this memoir will encourage the greatness of people from many paths in life.

Sometimes you walk the road less traveled by…alone. Alone in solitude but God is always there. God gives back so much more. Ideally, I was hoping Gloria would've lived to see this book – I would want her to be happy with it. Then again, it wouldn't have contained all the details I have written.

Three months after Gloria passed I went to Books a Million. I overheard a lady talking to the salesman: "I have a friend who has cancer, and I'm trying to find a book for her. I can't think of the title of the one I have in mind." I seized the moment,

"Ma'am, I couldn't help but overhear your conversation. There's a book I would highly recommend, *What Cancer Cannot Do.*" I stepped down the aisle next to her not expecting to find the book. It was the first book I laid my eyes on!

I reached out, pulled it off the shelf, and handed it to her. It was the only copy. I noticed how her expression lit up as she thanked me.

What is this message really about? Looking up – looking up to someone special who believes in you, and to God who sends that person to confirm your intended path. God reminds us that death is only a departure when He sends intuitive signs along the path.

Revisiting the Garden of Prayer is a sense of loyalty; although, I know Gloria isn't there. On Christmas Eve 2013 I left a, Whispers from Heaven, pewter angel wind chime where she is laid to rest. On Christmas day, there was a little pewter angel on my desk at work. Inscribed on this angel was the word *Faith*.

Don't ask me how it got there. No one knew about the angel wind chimes. I know logically speaking someone coincidently left it there. Metaphorically speaking,

I can take comfort in looking up and whisper... "Thank you Gloria." I'll be thinking of her too.

Life is not about weathering the storm –

it is learning to dance in the rain

TITLE: RONALD REAGAN A MAN Who Valued America

Specific goal statement: After my speech, I want my audience to believe Ronald Reagan's character made him a great president.

Thesis Statement: Ronald Reagan's character of integrity, duty, and hope set the stage for America's future.

Key: Character

Organizing Pattern: Claim of value

I. Introduction

A. Gaining attention: As a lifeguard Ronald Reagan saved 77 lives. The number is countless to how many American lives Ronald Reagan saved during his two presidential terms to the present day.

B. Connection: According to my class survey more than half of you know little about President Reagan, or know him by name only.

Only few believe that character can make political accomplishments, and many believe character doesn't really matter in a President

C. Credibility: I personally remember Ronald Reagan's powerful speeches. There's nothing more credible than Ronald Reagan's own words. I was eighteen when Ronald Reagan became the 40th President of the United States.

D. Preview: Ronald Reagan's character of integrity, duty, and hope set the stage for America's future by protecting freedom while courageously standing strong against adversity, won victory while achieving peace.

[First, let's review Ronald Reagan's character of Integrity]

II. Body

A. Reagan possessed a powerful integrity. He told American people the truth.

According to National Center,

1. Ronald Reagan addressed the ultimate danger America faced.

a. "The United States and the Soviet Union were the two superpowers aiming missiles of mass destruction that could, in a matter of minutes, destroy our society in which we live."

b. "A hundred years from now, will people look back and say Thank God for those people who headed off that loss of freedom and kept our world from nuclear destruction"?

2. Ronald Reagan valued American freedom.

   a. Ronald Reagan valued America's future generations.

   b. Ronald Reagan was a man who refused to give up on America!

[Next, we'll examine Ronald Reagan's character of Duty]

B. Reagan was willing to sacrifice popularity to do the right thing. According to an American Life by Ronald Reagan,

1. Ronald Reagan faced enormous opposition that he should go to Bitburg Germany.

   a. It was discovered forty-eight German SS were buried in the cemetery.

   b. Reagan, being a man of his word, refused to cancel the trip. He followed through with the ceremony, placing a wreath at the cemetery in Bitburg.

2. Ronald Reagan set an example that character is upheld through duty.

a. Reagan had a forgiving heart. He realized the German youth of the day were victims as those in the concentrations camps.

b. The next day ten-thousand Germans sung The Star Spangled Banner in perfect English.

[Third, I'll share the memory of Ronald Reagan's character of Hope]

C. Reagan would not leave unfinished business and gave America and the world a reason to hope.

According to the Reagan Foundation,

1. "June 12th, 1987 Reagan's speech at the Brandenburg Gate delivered to West Berlin was so audible President Reagan's words were heard by the people clear across to the east side of the Berlin wall".

    a. Reagan's message of hope was very clear. "General Secretary Gorbachev, if you seek peace, if you seek prosperity for the Soviet Union and Eastern Europe, if you seek liberalization: Come here to this gate!

Mr. Gorbachev, open this gate! Mr. Gorbachev, tear down this wall!"

    b. On November 9th, 1989 was a landmark in history. President Reagan lived to see East and West Berlin joined as one country the night the wall (after three decades) was torn down.

2. Reagan had meetings with Soviet leader Gorbachev on eliminating nuclear weapons.

According to History net,

    a. Reagan made it clear to Gorbachev "We can agree to either reduce or we can continue the arms race, which I think you know you can't win".

    b. On December 1987, for the first time in history, two superpowers agreed to eliminate an entire class of nuclear weapons. President Reagan had ended the Cold War.

[To sum up]

III. Conclusion

    A. Review: Ronald Reagan's character through his integrity, duty, and hope proved him to be a great leader who left a legacy for America to follow.

    B. Restate Connection: Now that you're familiar with Ronald Reagan, maybe you can see where character can and has made a tremendous difference for us today. We need to view today as yesterday's future, and the freedom we have from leaders who had us in mind. Today we need to focus on tomorrow and what kind of freedom we're leaving to our children, and grandchildren who will someday look back as today's pages will soon unfold in tomorrows' history.

C. Concluding Statement: I believe we're sitting here today because Ronald Wilson Reagan, a good man and great leader with noble character valued American Freedom. Ronald Reagan looked back two hundred years and proved the greatness America achieved once can be recaptured again. Today, I urge you to look back thirty years in history, and remember the character, courage, and boldness of Ronald Reagan, a character that can live on through future generations to restore America to greatness again.

In two years will be election time again. Today, we're at a very critical crossroads regarding America's future. It's imperative we focus strongly on the next President's character. A candidate whom will clearly define where he or she stands on the problems and issues, and what course of action must be taken for our nation. The decision is yours on what kind of government America is destined.

REFERENCES

President ronald reagan: *winning the cold war,* Retrieved from http://www.historynet.com/president-ronald-reagan-winning-the-cold-war htm

Reagan, R.W. (1990). *An american life*
New York, NY: Simon and Schuster

Reagan, R.W. (1976). *Remarks at the 1976 republican convention,* Retrieved from http://www.nationalcenter.org/reaganconvention 1976.html

Reagan, R.W. (1987). *Tear down this wall,* Retrieved from http://www.reaganfoundation.org/reagan/speeches/wall asp

*APPENDIX B

Rendezvous at Reykjavik

(A Look into the Character and Values of Ronald

Reagan and Mikhail Gorbachev)

I N THE MIDST OF THE most gigantic arms race in Cold War
History, President Reagan optimistically brainstorms an
innovative idea – The Strategic Defense Initiative (SDI) commonly
known as Star Wars. An Idea Reagan got from a movie titled Murder
in the Air. Initially, the experts ridiculed SDI by calling it Star Wars,
but more important SDI got the Soviet's attention.

This research began from a speech about Ronald Reagan presented
in Gloria Noble's class a year ago last fall. This led to an intriguing
research of the archives, Reagan's speeches, books from authors who
knew Reagan and Gorbachev, and the viewing of original footage of
Cold War events.

Among several eye-witnesses who hold diverse views on how the
Cold War ended, the character and values of both President Reagan

and General Secretary Gorbachev had a major impact in ending the Cold War.

C: Connection: Star Wars, a micro-chip laser space shield that would detect then eliminate oncoming nuclear missiles brought the leaders of two superpowers together in a heated debate at Reykjavik. The ultimate goal – eliminate nuclear missiles within ten years. Gorbachev feared SDI would give the U.S. first-strike initiative. He insisted President Reagan keep SDI in the laboratory. Reagan envisioned meeting with Gorbachev in ten-years and destroy the last nuclear weapon from the face of the earth. They came close to this agreement, but the word "laboratory" was edited from the papers. SDI was Reagan's insurance to discourage against an evil dictator in the future from rebuilding nuclear missiles.

President Reagan agreed to share his space-shield with the Soviets, but Gorbachev didn't believe him. At Reykjavik both leaders misperceived each other. The significance of the Reykjavik summit Reagan proved his character. He kept his word to the American people he would not trade off SDI. Both leaders picked up their papers and Reagan walked out on Gorbachev. Neither leader was very happy. It was ironic that Reagan, a former pacifist, ushered in an arms race with the Soviets. President Reagan suspected, yet would later realize, that Gorbachev, a proclaimed atheist, was a secret believer in God.

A. Preview: The research primarily focuses on the men – not the missiles. To compare the character and values of Ronald Reagan and Mikhail Gorbachev reveals that these leaders were men of truth, neither desired a nuclear war, and both men believed in freedom.

II. Body:

A. President Reagan and General Secretary Gorbachev displayed character and values of truth.

    1. Ronald Reagan spoke the truth about Communism while he fought it during his early years in Hollywood when he was President of the Screen Actors Guild and spokesman for Crusade for Freedom. According to National Center in spite of his defeat to Gerald Ford in 1976, Reagan launched off the greatest speech announcing to the American people, the truth of the danger we faced of "two superpowers aiming missiles of mass destruction which could in a matter of minutes destroy the society in which we lived. In the 1967 Town Hall Meeting of the World, Governor Reagan announced: To end the Cold War, the bridge had to be built on both sides.

    2. Twenty-years later, on the other side of the globe, the bridge was being built by a leader like no other Soviet leader before… Mikhail Gorbachev. One of Gorbachev's character traits, like Reagan's, according to A&E biography "he had a total

absence of fear to tell the truth when it wasn't told by others. In 1987, Gorbachev disclosed the Soviet's untold past history by revealing the Stalin purges and gulags. Gorbachev had Soviet history broadcasted to two-hundred million people. Gorbachev later told Michael Reagan: In order to rise to the Communist Party, he had to profess to be an atheist."

B. Neither leader desired a nuclear war

1. President Reagan clarified to reporter Marvin Kalb: "I've said this before to parliaments around the world, and I'll say it again today, a nuclear war cannot be won AND must never be fought."

President Reagan had a unique approach – Peace through Strength.

The Soviets, notorious for not keeping nuclear freeze agreements, Reagan decided to accelerate the arms race. Reagan stated: "This is why we are rebuilding our own strength. We must defend ourselves and make sure a war is never conceivable." Reagan displayed a balance of both characteristics by proclaiming the importance of saving lives when he announced SDI.

2. In 1985, at Geneva, Gorbachev confirmed to President Reagan, he didn't wake up every morning thinking about how he was going to take over the world nor expand Communism.

According to Kengor, Reagan suspected that Gorbachev was secret believer in God. Gorbachev commented to Reagan "We have never been at war with each other. Let us pray God that this never happens." (309).

C.   Both men believed in Freedom

1.   Years before Reagan thought of SDI, he proclaimed "There is no substitute for victory." Ronald Reagan believed in taking a stand for freedom, so future generations can enjoy that freedom through Democracy. According to Schweizer, "Reagan spoke about how freedom ultimately came from God and faith." Secretary of State George Shultz commented: "President Reagan set out to restore America – in the process he changed the world." In 1988 Reagan spoke to a group of Soviet students in Moscow "Even as we explore the most advanced reaches of science, we are returning to the age-old wisdom of our culture, a wisdom contained in the Book of Genesis in the bible. The key is freedom, freedom of thought, freedom of information, and freedom of communication." President Reagan once said: "Freedom is but one generation away from extinction." Ronald Reagan, the oldest president elected in American history left a legacy of freedom for the next generation.

2. Mikhail Gorbachev, the youngest Soviet leader to rise to power, was open to listen to what President Reagan had to say about Democracy. Gorbachev learned that people had religious rights under the U.S. Constitution, freedom to believe or not to believe. According to A&E biography, in 1988, Gorbachev persuaded Communists to back free-elections. A breath-taking televised event broadcasting the Soviets expressing open debates and freedom of speech.

Conclusion: Did Star Wars end the Cold War?

1. It is true that SDI brought the Soviets back to the table. Reagan took SDI out of the bargain by sharing it with different countries.

   In 1987 President Reagan and General Secretary Gorbachev signed the INF treaty eliminating an entire class of nuclear weapons. "Trust but Verify" became Reagan's motto when dealing with Gorbachev in future meetings. Gorbachev told Reagan: "You say that every time we meet."

2. However…if Star wars had existed in another era, it may not have had the same influence in ending the Cold War. Unlike Gorbachev, all former Soviet leaders had one goal in mind – to expand Communism throughout the world.

3. According to Kengor, most Russians believe Star Wars above all ended the Cold War. Other sources have gone so far as to call it luck.

4. SDI got the Soviets attention and brought two very unique and great leaders together.
   While Reagan held onto SDI and his promise to America, more important, Star Wars was in no way a substitute for the character and values of both Reagan and Gorbachev.

5. The Cold War ended because these two leaders were men of truth, they stood for peace, and both these men believed in freedom.

6. I just wonder what people would have said if they had only known, in a future era, that Ronald Reagan a former pacifist would usher in a gigantic arms race with a young Soviet leader, Mikhail Gorbachev a secret believer in God, and because of whom these two great leaders were, and together would end the Cold War?

BIBLIOGRAPHY

Books

Anderson, Martin, and Annelise Anderson. *Reagan's Secret War: The Untold Story of His Fight to Save the World from Nuclear Disaster.* New York: Crown Press, 2009.

Gorbachev, Mikhail. *Memoir.* New York: Doubleday Press, 1996.

Kengor, Paul. *The Crusader Ronald Reagan and the Fall of Communism.* New York: Harper Perennial Press, 2007.

Reagan, Micheael. *The New Reagan Revolution. How Ronald Reagan's Principles Can Restore America's Greatness.* New York: Thomas Dunne Books, 2001.

Reagan, Ronald. *An American Life.* New York: Simon & Schuster, 1990.

Noonan, Peggy. *When Character Was King.* New York: Viking Penquin Press, 2001.

Schweizer, Peter. *Reagan's War.* New York: Anchor Books, 2003.

Archives

Reagan, Ronald. "Address at Moscow State University." 1988. *http://millercenter.org/scripps/archives/speeches/detail/*3416 (8 August 2011).

Reagan, Ronald. *Talking Points Private Meeting With Shevardnadze.* Reagan Foundation Archives, 1985.

The Reykjavik File. *The President's First One-On-One Meeting With General Secretary Gorbachev.* Washington, D.C. 1986.

Shultz, George. *Cold War: Reykjavik* (Reagan-Gorbachev) *Summit (Shultz memoirs).* Margaret Thatcher Foundation. 1986.

Articles and Journals

Reagan, Ronald. "Remarks at the 1976 Republican Convention." *http://www.nationalcenter.org/reaganconvention 1976,html.* (accessed 3 October 2010).

Reagan, Ronald. "Tear Down This Wall." *http://www.reaganfoundation.org/reagan/speeches/wall* asp. (accessed 3 October 2010).

Reagan, Ronald. "Winning the Cold War." *http://www.historynet.com/president-ronald-reagan-winning-the-cold-war* htm.

Films and Speeches

A&E Biography Mikhail Gorbachev A Man Who Changed The World, dir. Mark Halliely (A&E Television Networks, 2002), DVD.

In The Face of Evil, dir. Stephen K. Bannon (Capital Films LLC, 2005), DVD.

Reagan, Ronald. *Speaking My Mind* (New York, NY : Simon & Schuster, 2004), CD.

Rise And Fall Of The Berlin Wall, dir. Oliver Halmburger (A&E Television Networks, 2009), DVD.